A Serious Call to a Contemplative Lifestyle

Revised Edition

A Serious Call to a Contemplative Lifestyle

Revised Edition

E. Glenn Hinson

Smyth & Helwys Publishing, Inc.
Macon, Georgia

Smyth & Helwys Publishing, Inc.
6316 Peake Road
Macon, Georgia 31210-3960
1-800-747-3016
©1993 by Smyth & Helwys Publishing
Second printing 1995
Third printing 2000
All rights reserved.
Printed in the United States of America.

E. Glenn Hinson

The paper used in this publication meets the mini-
mum requirements of American National
Standard for Information Sciences—Permanence
of Paper for Printed Library Materials. ANSI
Z39.48–1984. (alk. paper)

Library of Congress Cataloging-in-Publication Data

Hinson, E. Glenn
    A serious call to a contemplative lifestyle/ E. Glenn Hinson
    –Rev. ed.
    pp.   cm.
    Includes bibliographical references.
    1. Spiritual life—Christianity
    2. Contemplation
    I. Title.
    BV45001.2.H52 1993
    248.4'861—dc20

                                                    93-36037
                                                    CIP

ISBN 1-880837-40-4

Contents

Preface

This book has been written for students, especially collegians and seminarians. It began to take shape in 1970 as lectures for theological students at South Wales Baptist College, Cardiff, under the auspices of the Edwin Stephens Griffiths Foundation. It has developed further in retreats, conferences, and classes of various colleges and seminaries.

Students are my teachers. They may have taught me more than I have taught them.

They have taught me a lot about priorities and values. They have taught me about life-style. Today, the students with whom I am most closely associated, men and women at Baptist Theological Seminary at Richmond, are teaching me more and more about "the Beyond in the midst of our life." Some of them have assembled their own brainstorming (and heartstorming) groups in their houses and apartments, in the dormitories, and in local churches. They ask questions and they listen. They experiment with new styles of life, communes, forms of worship, modes of prayer.

In some sense, then, this book is feedback. As such, it is essentially a book about problems rather than about answers. It does not contain a handful of easy solutions for any problem of spirituality or devotion. What I should hope is that it will send you groping, along with my students and me, in the direction in which some answers may lie. If it does that, I will have received again the reward that students alone can confer on a teacher.

For the insights found in the book I am the debtor of many persons, some of whom I may credit by name and some of whom I may not. No one really recalls the host of those who shape his thought and experience. My spiritual formation began in a sort of "freethinkers" setting, with my earliest church memories being in a Spiritualist church, seances included. It grew next in the more regular and less speculative context of Baptist churches. For these years a saintly aunt and uncle taught me most about devotion, not by their words but by their lives. My subsequent formation has taken its biggest strides forward in moments of crises, much less by design than by coincidence. My awareness of God has been heightened in the "depths."

Still, the experiences in the depths have only supplied the matrix for growth. They could well have caused the stunting or even the shrinking of spirituality. That the latter did not happen I owe to the earlier foundations of faith and to the support of the church, not a particular congregation but the throng of people who belong to Christ's body—from my wife to colleagues in the Seminary to the saints down through the ages. Many of the insights, you may detect readily, have been found in the Christian devotional classics, through which I have guided students for several years. Just as these belong to the church universal, so also do many friends who have offered personal insights for this book: Thomas Merton, a Roman Catholic; Douglas Steere, a Quaker; Charles Whiston, an Episcopalian; and many others. Perhaps none of these friends will begrudge me the use of his thoughts so long as they prove beneficial to others.

E. G. H.
Richmond, Virginia

Chapter One

The Problems of
Devotion in the Space Age

An essay on the problems of devotion may be superfluous for those fortunate few who are entirely content with their present religious practice and experience. If you are one of those, you need not read farther.

These words are being written for those who do have problems, perhaps inarticulate and inarticulable but nevertheless real. In writing for these, who, I suspect, constitute the majority of believers in our day, I am writing for myself and about myself and my problems. And I will not apologize for the fact that I am raising more questions than I can answer here or elsewhere. We have passed through an era that sometimes boasted that it had all the answers. Let us hope that our own era is one where we have the integrity to keep our minds open to discern whether the answers are real or only pseudo answers.

To a large degree, our discernment and statement of problems depend upon what we mean by devotion. Some might circumscribe the word rather narrowly in terms of traditional devotional activities: prayer, Bible-reading, church attendance, retreats. Such a narrow definition would limit our task greatly, although the problems that each of these might raise are both vexing and numerous. Considered in this way, however, devotion would affect our lives only partially, partitioning them into neat rooms—here for religious, there for other activities. It is compartmentalization that the Old Testament prophets and our Lord inveighed against. What was it that Isaiah said? "Your new moons and your appointed feasts my soul hates; . . . cease to do evil, learn to do good; seek justice, correct oppression; defend the fatherless, plead for the widow" (Isa 1:14-17). Was this not Jesus' indictment of the religion of the Pharisees? They tithed mint, dill, and cummin but neglected the "weightier matters of the law" (Matt 23:23).

Devotion, then, if authentic, will encompass the whole of our lives. As I would define it, it has to do with the way in which I live out my faith commitment to God, the Father, who has manifested God's self and God's purpose uniquely in Jesus of Nazareth. Indeed, the Latin from which we take the word "devotion" means to vow or consecrate some-thing to the deity. In our case, then, devotional activities describe only a small patch in the whole plot of land. They are not unimportant, but they are important insofar as they contribute something to the enhancement and fulfillment of the larger commitment. In devotion we are talking about the living of life in view of our commitment to God.

The Surface Problem: Secularization

Given this definition, the place to begin probing for problems is in the area of life-styles. The modern life-style is a secular one, that is, one decreed largely by nonreligious motives and over which religious institu-tions have relatively little control. Most primitive societies have not distinguished between religious and secular motives. Consequently, in that context all activities have assumed religious overtones. It has been a trait of Western society, since the Middle Ages, to separate these as if they belonged to separate spheres. Indeed, the history of Western society has seen a gradual secularization whereby religion has been relegated to a smaller and smaller realm. Secularization, of course, has not proceeded at the same pace everywhere, but it has made steady and inexorable progress. In *The Modern Schism*, Martin Marty has pointed out that the triumph of the secular, visible around 1850, took different forms in Eu-rope, England, and America. In Europe it resulted in "utter secularity," where religion not only lost control but was attacked and suppressed. In England it achieved a less complete triumph that Marty has called "mere secularity." The church was not attacked so much as it was shrugged off. In America the outcome has been "controlled secularity," where religion has had limited roles assigned in public but has been relegated mostly to the private and personal *spheres.*

The impact of the secularization process upon devotion is easy enough to discern simply by comparing or contrasting the situation of the Christian in the church-dominated Middle Ages with that of the Christian in our own era.

In the Middle Ages all of life revolved around the church. the medieval church at the center of a village typified accurately the central place held by the church. The church spire commanded the terrain all around. All matters of consequence fell under its watchful gaze. Churches, monasteries, and religious buildings dotted the landscape.

The church set the clock. As the bells in the church tower tolled the third, sixth, and ninth hours of the day, devout Christians stopped to pray. Morning and evening they went to church to pray, sing, and listen.

The church regulated the calendar. Memorable occasions were "holy days." Whatever their origin—agriculture, pagan worship, or whatever else—they took on a significance in relation to a great moment in Christian history.

All matters of real importance in life, too, were debated and resolved by the church. If devout Christians got sick, they went to the priest to have prayers said and to have their heads anointed with oil. The priest was there in all the "rites of passage"—birth, adolescence, marriage, sickness, death, burial—ready to administer proper rites. The priest dispensed all necessary knowledge about things past, present, and future.

It is possible, of course, to exaggerate the control that the church may have exercised. Not every Christian, it need hardly be said, was devout— not even every monk, who was supposed to be a model for others, or cleric. But my concern here is to depict in broad strokes for the sake of contrast two contexts for living out Christian commitment. From this perspective what has been said is accurate enough to show the essentially religious drift of things. Most of persons' activities expressed their total commitment, devotion, because almost all activities had on them the stamp of the ecclesiastical institution. Whether they genuinely ended the dichotomy between religious and secular is debatable, but that question can be examined later.

It is obvious, to look at the modern era, that the secular city operates on another set of standards and with other institutions or forces in control. To discover what the standards and controlling forces are is one of the major problems of the modern metropolis, so I can hardly set these out. The economic motive, as Karl Marx pointed out, must be one of the most powerful. Masses still try to live by "bread" alone, but since our interest is in the impact that this has upon the life of devotion in today's world, we may confine our remarks to the areas mentioned with reference to the Middle Ages.

First, and an obvious point, the church as an institution is no longer the center of the metropolis as it was of the medieval village. Can you imagine a church steeple tall enough to be seen next to the Empire State

Building in New York City or the Sears Tower in Chicago? Indeed, medieval churches and cathedrals that once towered over great cities such as London or Paris, although they survive today, no longer hold their places of eminence. But this superficial example is indicative of a deeper truth about the dislocation of the church in metropolis.

The church no longer sets the clock, tolls the hours for workers, and calls the people of the community into its doors at will. In our highly technological setting, industry and commerce of varied descriptions do this. The industrial and commercial enterprise takes precedence over religious concerns in regards to the hours of the day. This means that Christian workers do not set their clocks by religious concerns. Rather, they have it set for them by the twenty-four-hours-a-day, seven-days-a-week, fifty-two-weeks-in-the-year industry or business for which they work. With a shortening of the individual workweek, some persons take extra full- or part-time jobs, so the schedule becomes even more complex.

The same process has enveloped the Christian calendar. Whereas the medieval church hallowed time for the constituents of its society, the modern church gives a weak witness to its special moments. To be sure, we still retain most of the formal designations and many of the dates of the calendar that the Middle Ages honored—Sunday, Christmas, and Easter, at least. But even these are falling. Sunday closing or "blue" laws, for example, are rapidly giving way under commercial pressures. And, what is of greater consequence, commercial interests create entirely different connotations for these special days. To a few, Christmas is a special day in honor of Christ's birth, but to nearly all it is a day for Santa Claus, for giving and receiving gifts. Likewise, Easter is less the day commemorating the resurrection of Christ than it is the day for the Easter bunny, decorated eggs, and new spring fashions. Even if devout Christians retain the proper nuances, they will have to yield to their employer in respect of observing these as "holy days." For industry and commerce will grind on, too expensive to close down, and they will fit their schedule. Their *religious* time is more negotiable than their *working* time.

Finally, there is the matter of authority. Obviously, the church's authority has been eroded in the four and a half centuries since the Protestant Reformation began. The locus of authority in modern society, being as diversified as it is, is not easy to determine. Generally speaking, however, today matters of real consequence in life are decided by "experts," by which we usually mean people of scientific and technological training. The amount of confidence, partly deserved, which Western society has put in science and in the university as the residence of science is immense. The scientist is consulted regarding fundamental and even ultimate questions of life and death. So much is this true that a Cambridge (England) scientist, Edmund Leach, boldly claimed in a *Look* magazine article, "We scientists have a right to play God." His point was: Scientists are already playing God in regard to creativity. They need merely take the next step to fill in the God gap by playing God in regard to morality. "God's major role is moral—He punishes (or redeems) the wicked. The scientist can now play God in his role as wonder-worker. . . . So we must now learn to play God in a moral as well as in a creative or destructive sense."[1]

For large numbers of people in Western society, science and its offspring, technology, do play God. They supply the "one thing needful." No better illustration of the shift from the church to science exists than the following: Upon his death an Arizona prospector willed a quarter of a million dollars to whoever could determine whether or not the soul lives on after death. The judge who probated the will decreed that the money should go not to a church, theological seminary, or religious organization of any sort, but to the nearest scientific institute. The decision is still being disputed, but the general tenor and implication of it are clear: Most persons, Christians included, will take their questions about life, death, and even the hereafter to the scientifically trained. The priest or minister no longer holds the ultimate solutions. And God, as Dietrich Bonhöffer wrote in *Letters and Papers From Prison*, is "edged out" a little farther from the center and toward the periphery of life. Certainly the church and religion are edged out to the periphery.

But we must not overstate the case here either, for there has been a widespread reaction to scientism, commercialism, and technocracy in the past several years. Youth especially have become disillusioned. A succession of problems—water and air pollution, the Watergate scandal, Chernobyl, the Iran-Contra Affair—have betrayed symptoms of a deeper malaise. Many reflective people now wonder whether Bonhöffer was premature in saying that humankind has "come of age," and whether scientists have earned a right to play God. True, the problems should not all be blamed on science, technology, industry, and commerce. But of those who have received much, much is expected.

The Root of the Problem: A Loss of Transcendence

The most salutary reaction to all of this has had a religious cast. In some instances, even the religious reaction has taken bizarre forms—demonology, witchcraft, astrology, Satanism, glossolalia, and similar phenomena. But there have been more reflective religious responses, too, which get at the root problem for devotion. Arnold Toynbee, the great historian of civilizations, in his book *Experiences*—published in his eightieth year —said that Western society, based on technology, poses the greatest threat to our survival as persons at any time since our ancestors became human. Whereas nature chastised us with whips, this new technological society we have created is chastising us with scorpions. Human hope lies in the world's religions, in helping us to recover the ground of being, in a change of heart.

Theodore Roszak, also a historian, has been doing an even more incisive critique of Western rationalism. The triumph of scientific orthodoxy, he argued, in *Where the Wasteland Ends*, has resulted in "the single vision." If all humankind hopes to survive, we must recover the powers of transcendence. For Roszak this would mean a return to the pre-Christian era, to gnosis, and to the personalistic model of reality that existed there. Roszak, a former Catholic, blames orthodox Christianity for science, so the hope lies in getting behind science and behind Christianity.

Toynbee and Roszak have struck the problem at its center. Are Western persons capable any longer of experiencing transcendence? Or have they reached the point in their rationalism, scientism, and technologism that their spirit has wasted and atrophied so much as to make the intuitive approach impossible? As Father Alfred Delp queried in his *Prison Meditations*, are modern persons fit for religion and for God?

These questions cannot be easily answered, and we who believe must not smile smugly as if our experience would answer for everybody else. The fact is that our technocratic society complicates immensely the experience of transcendence. For one thing, it inhibits the experience of personal, individual self-transcendence. The metropolis, for all the benefits it brings us, depersonalizes. People become things, objects, nameless entities, IBM numbers, dog tags, ID bracelets. This is due, among other things, to the rapid pace of change so well described by Alvin Toffler in *Future Shock*. Things, places, people, information, organizations—all are transient and impermanent. They are disposable. We use them and discard them. It is due also to size. Although Harvey Cox, in *The Secular City*, lauded the anonymity of the metropolis for the freedom it permits, many others have questioned it. Ashley Montagu, a noted sociologist, has challenged the whole urban trend. It is his contention that urban life "is really incompatible with humanity." He does not believe that human beings can retain their identity as human beings in cities larger than a few thousand. Small communities alone allow people to become deeply involved in one another's lives.[2]

If the city causes a loss of perception in regard to personal self-transcendence, it causes an even greater loss of perception in regard to divine transcendence. In the metropolis, people witness the handiwork of human beings, seldom the handiwork of God. They see more and more brilliantly engineered buildings, bridges, and highways, fewer and fewer trees, lawns, and flowers. They experience more and more of human commerce in food, clothing, and pleasure, less and less of the beauty of sun, moon, and stars. In baseball and football stadiums that use artificial turf we have at last achieved a total victory over nature. In doing so, however, we have paid an increasingly greater price in our experience of transcendence, even our own self-transcendence.

Unfortunately education has not helped here. The university has been taken over more and more by science and technology, largely because that is where the federal and state stipends are. And university presidents know as well as anyone that "the one who pays the piper calls the tune." Universities operate on the rationale of supplying "knowledge for use." They serve the public and meet public demands. Since the public has demanded more science and technology, they have concentrated on these. In 1964, for example, 97 percent of all federal grants went to the technological (40%), medical (37%), and physical (20%) sciences; only 3 percent went to the social sciences; none went to the humanities. The humanities would conserve something of the intuitive, artistic, and poetic approach to life, but, for most universities, they have become little more than excess baggage.[3]

Can we hope that there will be a swing of the pendulum? Such a swing, I think, is in evidence already in some of the restlessness and turmoil of the age, which, incidentally, has many correspondences to the troubled fourth century C.E. in Roman history. Are these movements not rather confused affirmations of Augustine's famous confession, "Our heart is restless until it finds rest in Thee"?[4] Many state this explicitly— the "now generation" with their contempt for the past, the hippies with their rejection of our current life-style, the myriad religious and quasi- religious cults that are seeking "experience" of God, those vast numbers now turning to transcendental meditation (TM) and Eastern religions, and experimenters with mind-expanding drugs and potions of one type or another. There is an even more reflective confirmation of this truth in the Communist-Christian "dialogue." The now excommunicated French Marx- ist Roger Garaudy, among others, has called attention to the failing of modern Communism to take transcendence into account. And it is this element to which he urges Christians to bear their witness.[5]

The Trappist monk Thomas Merton perceived this unmet longing of modern persons in the immediate post-World War II era when he found his books on contemplation read avidly by people everywhere. As he explained the problem near the end of his life, human beings have an instinctive desire for peace and tranquillity, for harmony. But our modern life-style is doing anything but giving us that. To the contrary, it im- merses us in activity for its own sake, scientism, the cult of unlimited power, the worship of the machine as an end in itself.[6] The fact that meaninglessness was so much an observable and apparently inherent phenomenon in Western culture was what drove Merton farther and far- ther in a study of Eastern culture, especially religions. "Western man needs oriental wisdom," he argued as early as 1962. We need to seek truth for its own sake, to discover again the ground of being, to come to ourselves.[7]

The problem stated here may have been multiplied many times over by the belief that, via science and technology, we have at last "come of age." To be sure, we have to have a certain amount of confidence in our rational powers, but by placing total confidence in them we have made ourselves a prisoner of our own technology. Technology demands more technology. As Toffler put it, "it feeds on itself."[8] Thus a whole culture has gone out of control, the machine threatening to annihilate its maker. Whether this destruction would come by some Orwellian holocaust or as in Huxley's *Brave New World* does not matter. It only matters that today, despite superficial signs of "freedom," you and I do not seem able to choose our life-styles. One we do not like and do not want is imposed upon us. It is locking out our perception of the transcendent and crushing the sense of the personal.

The Underlying Problem:
How Do We See God in the Picture?

Further complicating the practical problems described above is a conceptual problem. Although concepts are not necessarily the deepest motive for behavior, they do influence and affect other motives. What we believe may affect our behavior subconsciously. And if we wish to alter the conditions that influence our behavior, we need to deal with ideas.

The conceptual problem I am pointing out is not an easy one with which to deal in a conservative American religious context, for it has to do with the relationship between Biblical faith and a scientific world view. Briefly stated, the issue is this: Accepting the scientific picture of the universe and of human existence, how do we see God, as revealed in the historical events recorded in the Scriptures, fitting into the picture?

Many devout persons, I realize, may decline an invitation to work out a reconciliation. They may profess to be content with the world view given in the Scriptures and thus they feel they do not have to adjust their understanding of God.

The trouble with making no effort to effect a reconciliation, as subsequent chapters will show more fully, is that it results in a kind of religious schizophrenia, the compartmentalization of our thought and activities into "religious" and "secular" categories. To be sure, the biblical world view may not have caused compartmentalization for people prior to the Renaissance, as it does for us, for it genuinely represented both their everyday and their religious world view. Most of us, however, have another world view by which we think and act daily, one fashioned by modern science. In our society the person who refuses to function under the authority of the scientific is a rarity. A noteworthy example would be the devout adherents of "faith" sects who refuse medical attention on religious grounds. In doing so, they are at least consistent. But the same is not true of persons who accept the scientific view in most areas but make no effort to decide what bearing this has on their religious commitment. For those areas they plead "King's X" with God. Their devotion is something that they do or have done to them. It does not represent the working out of their commitment to God in all of life. It is playacting at religion, doing exercises to be seen of them rather than to serve God.

For most of us, then, it is crucial to reconcile, whether successfully in all respects or not, the biblical perspective and the scientific perspective. Each of these will be authoritative for us to whatever extent it rings true to our experience. The scientific will be authoritative in those realms where its empirical observations ring true. The biblical will be authoritative in those realms where its spiritual insights ring true. Methodologically it is almost inevitable that we will begin with the empirical, that which is arrived at by sensory observation. This means that we will accept all that science demonstrates empirically. Because we believe, however, we will not stop there. Our faith compels us to ask questions as to *how* all these fragmentary bits derived from empirical observation fit together in some integrated whole. Note that we do not ask *whether* they do, but how. It is our prelogical supposition that they do. According to this presupposition, it is God who integrates all of them, brings all of them into a coherent and meaningful pattern.

The integrative task that faces the believer can be stated in terms of several traditional dichotomies: sacred versus secular, natural versus supernatural, here versus hereafter, and immanent versus transcendent. To some extent, all represent slightly different angles of approaching the same fundamental question, viz., how we visualize God fitting into the picture of our existence. Because we use all four approaches from time to time, it will be useful to give some attention to each.

First of all, in regard to the sacred and the secular, how does God relate to different things, places, people, times, organizations, and so on? Does God regard some of these as holy, consecrated to God, whereas others are not, as traditional religious practice has frequently suggested? Thus we have had holy objects, holy places, holy persons, holy seasons, and holy church delineated by symbols of consecration. To set apart certain things, for example, the priest invoked God's special blessing, sprinkled them with holy water, and declared them off limits to secular usage. Or sometimes they were set apart in more casual ways. A church building, for example, became "God's house" in such a way that other activities were forbidden there. How many pastors have discovered extreme and adamant opposition when they suggested using church buildings for "secular" activities—day care programs, weekday kinder-gartens, neighborhood recreational programs, and others?

On the opposite extreme, some have asked whether we should not eliminate all distinctions. If religious people are inclined to dichotomize, why not say either that all things are sacred and nothing is secular or that nothing is sacred and all things are secular? The first point of view is advocated by the Quakers. Why have *two* sacraments, they ask, when all things may be sacramental? The second point of view is advocated by a wide segment of devotees of secularity. Is not everything simply what it appears to be? If so, can we distinguish one object, place, person, organ-ization, etc., except by its personal value to us individually?

Second, in regard to the natural and the supernatural, how does God relate to the natural order of things? Shall we believe that God intervenes in human events at will, as popular religious behavior and thought often suggest? According to this view, God lets nature run its course until we get into trouble and call out for help; then God intervenes *super*-natu-rally. Several years ago, for instance, a faith-healing group claimed that God had granted (one could hardly say restored) eyesight to a boy born without eye sockets. Or, from the opposite side, shall we say that God is totally bound by the natural order of things? Hence, in the mind of the seventeenth-century Deists, all things run in the manner of a clock and God does not intervene. What will be will be, even for God. Or, as an alternative, shall we say that God, foreknowing all that would happen, prearranged everything according to divine foreknowledge? Thus even God's interventions—for example, the miracle of the Red Sea crossing —are prearranged. Although God does not deviate from the plan set forth from the beginning, God does display power over nature.

Third, in regard to the here and the hereafter, what is the relationship between life now and life after death? Shall we envision a sharp line of demarcation at death so that life here is both qualitatively and quanti-tatively different from life hereafter? This, too, has been typical. In the harsh Middle Ages the church accentuated the glories of the life beyond at the expense of present human existence. The medieval person's song could well have been, "The world is not my home,/I'm just a passin' through,/My glories are laid up/Somewhere beyond the blue." The present is to be endured, not enjoyed. Let us, therefore, not waste time trying to improve what is only temporary; let us get on with that which really matters. Or shall we, taking the opposite side, say: "This life is all. Let us enjoy it while we have time, since we know nothing of life hereafter"? Both overtly and covertly many are doing this.

Finally, in regard to immanence and transcendence, how can we conceive of God as at one and the same time intimately involved in the universe and yet not simply equivalent to it? Shall we conceive of God's immanence or transcendence *spatially*, as the primitive world view did? God is normally "up there," high above all earthly realities. Occasionally, God becomes immanent "down here" in order to set creation right again. Or, on the opposite extreme, shall we say God is totally immanent, as some secular theologians argue? What we describe in regard to the natural order is God's action. God is wholly within the secular process. Thus there is no need to think of transcendence at all.

The real crux of the God problem for modern persons, including the other dichotomies, undoubtedly comes to a focus in the question of immanence and transcendence. The real issue is whether, given the dominance of the scientific world view, we can fit the personalistic conception of God as depicted in the Scriptures into the framework supplied by modern science. Some are content to let the "God-hypothesis" fade out of the picture. Since retaining this hypothesis involves great difficulties, they counsel that we should not belabor modern persons with it. It will be more beneficial to them if we live as exemplary human beings and help them to live as they should.

I cannot agree, even if I can appreciate the motives behind this approach. For one thing, one could hardly render a greater disservice to secular persons than to let them rest comfortably in the fallacious assumption that theirs is the best of all possible worlds and that nothing more can be added. I agree with the oft-quoted remark of Voltaire: "If there were no God, man would have to invent one." Indeed, we do so continually. Out of fear, if for no other reason, we deify the proximate and the temporary. Fearful persons do not ask whether something is safe before they grab hold. They just grab it. This point is graphically illustrated in the popular movie *The Poseidon Adventure*. Shortly after the ship capsized, the minister tried to lead the survivors to the thinnest part of the hull, where they might be rescued most easily. A few followed him. Most refused. They clung mightily to the temporary security of the ballroom, where they were gathered to wait for rescue.

No service will be rendered modern persons, therefore, by affirming their tenacious grasp upon proximate realities. The fact is, as Father

Alfred Delp stated so well in an Advent message, human life, by its very nature, requires both purpose and fulfillment, neither of which are salient features of Western civilization at the moment. The meaninglessness of our society has been portrayed graphically by Nobel Prize-winning playwright Samuel Beckett in *Endgame* and in many other plays. One Beckett play consists of a pile of rubble that the audience stared at for fifteen minutes before it was bulldozed away. But he could hardly speak more eloquent and stark testimony than the thousands who take their own lives, "cop out" on alcohol and drugs, wither away inwardly, or die prematurely for lack of purpose. The proximates that masses today are substituting for ultimates—money, jobs, houses, cars, athletic contests, sexual license, insurance policies, the state, even the institutional church—are not supplying an instinctive deeper requirement of human existence.

Ultimately it is this deeper need to which we are answerable, that within our own nature that has to return to its source. Within each of us there is a homing instinct. It is possible for us to suffer temporary displacement, but eventually our instinct drives us back to our home. It is our homing instinct, surely, which sends us in great droves to rediscover nature. Perhaps also it is our homing instinct that will send us to rediscover God as the ground of our being.

Chapter Two

God's Place in the Picture

If our devotion is going to have greater meaning, we will have to do an infinitely better job than we now are conceptualizing the way in which God fits into the picture of our personal existence.

This is not an issue that we can dismiss with a glib and easy answer, for it involves the most fundamental question with which a believer must wrestle. It concerns the tension between our daily existence and our religious commitment. Daily we depend upon science for our understanding of things, places, and people; religiously we depend upon the Scriptures. How can we bring these two together so that our commitment to the God who has disclosed God's self through the events recorded in the Scriptures will bear upon our daily lives in their totality, not just in this or that compartment?

There may be more than one satisfactory answer to the latter question. An individual's answer will depend upon personal background and orientation. The challenge, however, is to frame an understanding of God that will integrate our everyday thoughts and behavior with our religious thoughts and behavior and thus bridge the chasm that often separates our everyday and our religious worlds. To meet the challenge, we will have to satisfy both an intellectual and an experiential or psychological frame of reference, for we respond to our worlds both rationally and intuitively.

Some Inadequate Solutions

Let us begin by looking at two antipathetic solutions that are influential today.

One of these is to rely wholly on the Scriptures for one's scientific as well as one's religious understanding and activity. This would mean a world view somewhat as follows: The earth is a flat plate set upon pillars over a watery chasm. The firmament stretches over it like a giant bowl. From the firmament, which separates the waters above the earth from the waters below, hang sun, moon, and stars. Heaven is "up there" above the firmament, hell "down there" in the bowels of the earth. God sits on a throne in the upper heavens and directs events below. When God wishes it to rain, God opens the windows of heaven and lets the water pour down. God intervenes in human events from time to time as needed; otherwise, God oversees it with watchful eye. This world is, at most, ten thousand years old. It came into existence by a seven-day fiat. Soon it will end as God grows tired of the wicked doings of humankind. Jesus will descend out of heaven in the reverse of his ascension to usher in the climactic event.

Some very devout persons try to live consistently by this world view, and one may not gainsay the strength and integrity of their commitment. But the problems in retaining such a position are too obvious to gloss over. For one thing, the flat earth theory is difficult to sustain in the face of the modern space shots that have relayed back to the earth pictures of a globe. For another, the idea of waters surrounding the earth does not correspond to our experiences of space. For another, the seven-day creation theory is hard put to explain fossils, radiocarbon tests of the age of the earth, and many other data now supplied by highly sensitive scientific instruments.

Science, to be sure, has to make modest claims for its theories. The broader the hypotheses, the greater the chance of error. Consequently, there are variant theories of evolution. But the possibility of error in framing broad theories does not negate the reliability of basic empirical data. And science is its own best critic. It hardly suffices, therefore, to toss aside empirical data by charging scientists with deception ("They just put those pictures on television to fool people") or by ascribing counter-deceptions and incredible miracles to God ("God put those fossils in the earth to fool scientists," or "If Jesus turned water into wine, God could age the earth all at once so that it could seem billions of years old"). It is wiser to accept demonstrated data and to leave the framing of scientific hypotheses to those who have the training, instruments, and methods to do so accurately.

Whether consciously or subconsciously, most people in Western society accept the guidance of science for everyday matters. They consult doctors, engineers, pharmacists, and the myriad other "specialists." To do so, however, without making a corresponding adjustment in their religious lives creates the dichotomy that underlies religious hypocrisy or compartmentalization. God enters the picture only in part, and that the small part. God is the Sunday friend and the "troubleshooter," not the center of all of life. God is, at best, a marginal element in our existence.

In reaction to this kind of compartmentalization some theologians have gone to the opposite extreme. Better to take the scientific rationale and to leave God out of the picture altogether than to live with a dichotomy.

The first Christian thinker to pose this alternative rather pointedly was Dietrich Bonhöffer, hanged by the Nazis shortly before he would have been liberated by American troops. Bonhöffer, doubting whether Westerners could use a "God-hypotheses" any longer, having "come of age" in their scientific sophistication, speculated that God was perhaps withdrawing in order that we might learn how to get along in the world without God. God lets God's self be "edged out," placed on a cross, so that we can live as if God did not exist.[9]

The "God is dead" theologians carried this thought to its logical extreme. The more radical pair of them, Thomas J. J. Altizer and William Hamilton, seized upon Nietzsche's famous phrase and applied it to Bonhöffer's thought. In their primitive state human beings needed God and religion to cope with their insecurities. Gradually, however, they have "come of age." In Jesus, rightly interpreted, God finally made our independence possible. God literally poured God's self into the life of a man and died. Now God is no more. What we have to do is to live with the absence of God that we all are experiencing. This means that we will live fully human lives.

The kind of life this would entail has been portrayed in Allen R. Brockway's *The Secular Saint*. The "secular saint" recognizes that religious language has little meaning in a "steady state world" such as ours. This world is "bereft of religion." God is, after all, a projection of our own selves. The Father, Son, and Spirit of traditional Christian thought are useful in explaining how we interact with our world. God is "definition," the limits of human capacities; Christ is "possibility," the fearless stepping forth into the unknown; and the Holy Spirit is "decision, a man's own decision to receive the Christ possibility, the only life-giving possibility." The three persons of the Trinity are, for us today, "symbolic ways of apprehending the reality of their relationships with the world around them—and at the same time affirming a particular character for that relationship."[10] Secular saints can live without a God-hypothesis; their faith is in themselves. They have everything under control at all times. They do not need the church and religious symbols, though they may put up with them. Indeed, if they go down in an airplane crash, their final agonizing thought is not God nor their own survival but whether they took care of the insurance premiums so that their family will be properly provided for. Shades of Nietzsche's "superman"!

Radical theologians cited one persuasive argument in support of their view—the experience of God's absence in the modern day. Indeed, some less-radical representatives of "God is dead" theology—Paul van Buren and Gabriel Vahanian—were concerned primarily with describing this phenomenon. Even if God exists, they argued, modern persons are no longer capable of thinking of God as God. In Bonhöffer's words, the "God-hypothesis" is dead. Modern persons' "God-consciousness" has atrophied. So there is no use trying to talk to them any longer as if God did exist. Rather, let us talk to them in language they can understand, namely, about themselves and about concern for others.

Much can and will be said later in appreciation of the concern of radical theology for humankind and particularly for its emphasis on social concern. Furthermore, the church owes a debt to Bonhöffer and his tribe for laying bare the deeply rooted problem of communicating with modern persons about God. Even if they exaggerated the scope of the problem, they put the problem itself in bold relief.

The difficulty with what they proposed was not in diagnosis but in prescription. The prescription was more radical than the disease. To cure deafness, as it were, they recommended the cessation of speech. The fact that modern persons are not experiencing God any longer does not prove, after all, that God does not exist. It proves only that we have a problem. Should we, then, in response to this problem cease trying to restore an atrophied member by some kind of therapy? This is not to say that we should go on repeating ancient cliches as if eventually they will be heard. A lot of new approaches and new language need to be put to work. But ceasing to use God-language altogether will do no more than allow the experience of God to slip farther beyond the horizon.

What should be done would appear to me to lie in the very opposite direction from that proposed by radical theology. The first step is, as Father Alfred Delp said in the *Prison Meditations*, to "restore man to a state of fitness for God and religion."[11] This restoration will require a significant redirection of our current approach to education. Instead of continuing to augment the rational capacities, we need to cultivate the intuitive capacities, the powers of transcendence, as Theodore Roszak calls them, the sensitivities of the artist and the poet. I am not suggesting in this proposal an abandonment of the rational, as some have, but the restoration of a balance. Human experience itself surely does not confirm the theory that human beings are purely rational creatures who process their experiences solely in the mind. Even the scientist "knows" by intuition as well as by observation and reflection.[1] The challenge, then, would appear to be to enhance our imaginations, our sense of wonder, our creative capacities in such a way as to take them beyond reason and observation. The "twilight zone" may hold many mysteries that our rationalism may not have ferreted out.

Once we have regained some balance between the rational and the intuitive capacities, we may become capable of understanding God-language again. This seems to be precisely what is happening in the multifaceted religious revival of the present. There are irrational and anti-rational elements in this revival, but, in the main, the quest is for the suprarational, for something that will bring a meaning and an order to life that the dominant rationalism and scientism of the day are failing to supply. Is it so remarkable really, when one discerns this concern, to hear voices of former skeptics such as Malcolm Muggeridge, the urbane BBC interviewer and critic, claim to have rediscovered the mystical aura of Jesus while filming a four-part series on the life of Jesus in Palestine?[13] The musical *Jesus Christ Superstar* expresses the sentiment of many seekers today: "He's only a man, but. . . ." The authors of this play profess no religious commitment, but their play leaves an unanswered question, a mystery that the Gospel writers would approve. Whether or not any of these persons come out with a conventional and "orthodox" theology, they are showing, I think, that human capacity for religion and for God is still there; it just needs to be recovered and used. Radical theology was too quick to throw in the towel to the current life-style and modes of thought. Had it held sway for long, radical theology would have magnified rather than diminished the plight of persons in the secular city. One welcomes, therefore, some new sounds from representatives of radical theology. For example, Harvey Cox has been saying things that clash with his earlier hymn of praise to *The Secular City*.[14] In *The Feast of Fools* he lauded medieval fantasying. In *The Seduction of the Spirit* he discovered the charismatic movement. Later he suggested *Turning East* to oriental religion.

God and Process

The theology that appears to me to offer the best metaphysical framework for conceptualizing the way in which God fits into the picture is the evolutionary theology of Teilhard de Chardin. Its strength is that it begins with a world view supplied by modern science and shows how Christian faith addresses itself to humankind against that backdrop. This is the correct order, for it is the scientific world view that, whether consciously or subconsciously, dominates our self-understanding. We can escape it only by turning our normal patterns of thought upside down or by ignoring them. These patterns are etched upon our minds from childhood through the educational processes of our society—television, newspapers, books, schools, and all the rest. We cannot eradicate them.

There are different schools of process theology. The American school goes back to Alfred North Whitehead and includes scholars such as Charles Hartshorne, Norman Pittenger, John Cobb, Daniel Day Williams, Shubert Ogden, and Eric C. Rust. However, the person who has shaped my own thought most was the great Jesuit paleontologist and philosopher Pierre Teilhard de Chardin. During his lifetime, Teilhard was not allowed to publish any of his theological writings because of their explosive implications for church doctrine. He spent most of his lifetime in China in field excavation. Since his death in 1955, however, a flood of his compositions have poured from the presses. His thought had a significant impact on the Second Vatican Council. It has figured prominently in the Christian-Marxist dialogue in Europe, Marxists being particularly partial to it. No single thinker since Thomas Aquinas, who, ironically, was also suspect during his career and for a time after his death, has promised to exert a greater impact on Christian thought than Teilhard. This impact will doubtless be a broad one, but in no area will it be more significant than in the area of spirituality or devotion.

Teilhard's theology has been criticized at several points, and, like any far-reaching system, it does have weaknesses, some of which he himself recognized. Some scientists have questioned his evolutionary schema as a whole, but it has had approval from others. The most glaring deficiency, it seems to me, is its failure to take the problem of evil, particularly deliberate human evil, with proper seriousness. This is a consequence of the fact that Teilhard focused so much on the long sweep of evolution that he neglected history. History does not leave room for his incredible optimism. At times his letters gloss over the tragic aspects of human events, like death in battle, with a redundant "Cheer up—and some day all will be well." There are weaknesses, too, in his handling of the personal. The individual is lost to view in the evolutionary sweep. Although humankind is "the arrow" pointing the way to the goal of the process, "evolution become conscious of itself," its particular significance as persons is not explained. More particularly, the individual's future is considered as a part of the future of humankind, not as an individual and personal entity. Furthermore, Teilhard did not emphasize enough the critical threshold that separates human beings from the chain of their predecessors and from nature. In the face of ecological crises, to be sure, we owe Teilhard a word of thanks for reminding us of our continuity with and dependence upon nature. He himself loved "earth's blind matter," as his chief biographer and friend, Claude Cuenot, says.[15] But humankind has a uniqueness to which Teilhard paid too little heed.

What this means is that, though we may take the basic model from Teilhard, we will want to supplement, adjust, and correct it with other theological insights. More traditional Christian theology, for example, will accentuate more heavily a realistic view of evil, viz., that human beings, for all their capabilities, are sinners. Existentialism, likewise, offers insights into the personal dimension of our existence. Such theologies, however, need not conflict of necessity with the broad metaphysical model that Teilhard provided. What these will do is to sharpen the general scheme.

Teilhard, not being a physicist, sidestepped the issue of the origins of the universe as a whole, and we shall do so here also. He began with matter. Even at this level, he insisted, there is "consciousness." The evolutionary process began with an infolding or "involution" of the Without (outer shell) upon the Within (inner consciousness). Then, by "aggregation" of simple units, more complex forms came into existence. Over millions upon millions of years the evolutionary process has passed through three stages—from the geosphere (the level of matter) to the biosphere (the level of animate life) to the noosphere (the level of mind).

It is this third stage that supplies a clue to the whole process, and it is significant that Teilhard entitled his *magnum opus* on evolution *The Phenomenon of Man*. The whole process may be called "hominization" —progress toward humankind. But man's human evolution is pointing to something beyond humankind, which implies something much more wonderful than we once thought about ourselves, that is, that we were the center of the universe. We are distinguished from the animal not merely by the fact that we know. We have not merely consciousness but self-consciousness. We know that we know. Thence we are able to participate in the evolutionary process, to direct it forward and upward to its goal.

Teilhard called the goal to which the evolution of humankind points the Omega-point. Omega is the hyperpersonal, the One, the ultimate in consciousness. The whole process does not proceed forward by a "push" from below. Such a push would be inadequate to explain the gradual progress toward self-consciousness. Rather, it is pulled forward from above, from the Omega-point. The forward march is, of course, not a steady one. Just as there is a pull from Omega, so there is a pull backward by forces of dissolution. Thus there may be three steps forward and four backward, five forward and two backward, and so on. But the pull from Omega is stronger than the forces that work against it.

The force that fills the universe and moves it forward toward itself is not an impersonal one. It is the force of love, of the hyperpersonal.

In the main body of *The Phenomenon of Man*, Teilhard made no attempt to relate his scientific hypothesis to Christian faith. Indeed, Julian Huxley, the famous biologist, who is a professed agnostic, was able to express essential agreement with it in the preface that he wrote to *The Phenomenon of Man*. The points of conjunction, however, are discernible and, in an appendix, Teilhard pointed out some of them; in other writings he amplified further.

Teilhard was convinced that "the sceptics, agnostics, and false positivists are wrong. Within all this shift of civilization, the world is neither moving at random nor marking time; beneath the universal turmoil of living beings, something is being made, something heavenly, no doubt, but first something temporal."[16] God, who is love, fills all things and yet pulls the universe forward and upward toward God's self. In the course of human evolution this love has left clues. In Jesus of Nazareth love gave the ultimate clue. Indeed, the whole process may be called "Christogenesis," viz., evolution toward Christ. Christ is what humanity is becoming. Ultimately humankind is evolving toward God's self. One day, to quote Paul in 1 Cor. 15:28, God will be "all in all."

It is in this way that Teilhard supplied a solution to the basic problem of God's immanence and transcendence. God's transcendence is not spatial but personal and futuristic. God is within all and through all and yet beyond all (Col 1:15-20). Put another way, love fills all things and yet is greater than all. Love controls and gives direction to all.

Because Teilhard's view is so personalistic, it may be helpful to use myself as an analogy. As a person, you may see all of me. I am wholly immanent within my physical body—from head to toe and from fingertip to fingertip. Yet I am more than you can see also. I possess self-transcendence. I can interact with myself. I can interact, too, with other persons and with my environment. Above all, I am conscious of my own existence as a person.

To be sure, this analogy breaks down, as all analogies do. Whereas I am one among many persons, God is unique. It is appropriate that we speak of God not as "*a* person" but as "person." God is the "I am," existence itself, "besides whom there is no other." God encompasses the boundaries of all existence, including God's own. So God's interaction will not be with things outside those boundaries but within God's self. This is not to say, as pantheists would, that God *is* all things or, conversely, that all things are God. It is to say that God is *within* all things and that all things are within God. In the words of the Apostle Paul, "in God we live and move and have our being." This view is known as *panentheism*, that is, that God is *within* all things.

This view raises an intriguing question about the possibility of God's own development. Traditional theology has emphasized God's immutability or unchangeableness. What is called apophatic (negative-way) theology laid out a whole list of negatives, formed in reverse of human analogies. If, however, we follow the logical conclusion of the evolutionary model, then we have to say that, as God directs the process of evolution, God adds to God's self. How can we conceive this?

We cannot say, of course, that the *boundaries* of God's existence grow bigger, for God always encompasses all that is. Rather, to come back to our personal model, God adds to God's own personal being. God is all that God will be and yet God is becoming. *Potentially* God has always been perfect love. What God adds to this potential, however, is the reality. Thence in the creative process God adds to God's own self the fulfillment of a potential as creator; in the redemption of humankind God adds to God's own self the fulfillment of God's potential as redeemer. The development of God's creation in the direction that God purposes for it, therefore, redounds to God's glory in the sense of complementing God's divine personhood.

This is not to dispute God's perfection. God's love is perfect. But personal perfection does not negate the possibility of growth. Is it not the essence of the personal to grow? In fulfilling God's potential as person, therefore, God is acting in accordance with God's own personal nature.

The Will of God for Us

This discussion of the personal model of God brings us to the central question for devotion from the human perspective, namely, the will of God and human freedom.

In the seventeenth century the spatial concept of transcendence led Deists, whose thought had a profound influence on America's Founding Fathers, to frame a picture of God as the celestial clockmaker. God made the world like a clock, flung it into space, and let it run by itself. This means that the universe operates in predictable, mechanical fashion, that is, according to natural law. Human freedom lies, as the ancient Stoics proposed, in meshing human activities and desires with the inexorable laws. To be happy, one should live "reasonably."

In America this has received a Calvinistic twist that has strengthened the determinism of it. Although Calvin himself conserved an element of human freedom, his heirs have sometimes projected a highly particularized predestination in which they have seen God causing everything that occurs, even evil. God foreknows; therefore, God causes to happen. The harshness of life in America, first in the colonial era and later on the frontier, let this be forged into an iron rule. If anything happened, happy or tragic, "it was God's will."

The question that one has to put to this conception of God is whether it allows adequate room for human freedom, such as the Scriptures and our own experience suggest. A more personal understanding of God, as suggested by process theology, would allow room for human beings to exercise a full range of options. In other words, it would be conceivable that more than one thing could be God's will in a particular set of circumstances.

To be sure, there are some either/ors. One certainly is the decision we make with reference to God. There may also be certain moral decisions that, in certain circumstances, approach an either/or. However, most of our decisions involve a wider range of choices. They may be graded over a spectrum that might leave many of them desirable and appropriate. Actually, one only knows in *retrospect* whether a choice was right, "according to God's will." In making the choice, one has to exercise responsibility. The more intelligent and able a person is, the more options he/she is likely to have. But, for most of life's decisions, few persons are faced with only a right and wrong choice. Is it not possible, for instance, that a person could choose more than one from a number of persons as an appropriate life partner? Or is it not possible that one could fulfill God's will in more than one occupation? I think so.

This decrees, then, that we abandon the model of the clockmaker and substitute another. The one that I think does proper justice to human freedom is that of the chess master. After the first few moves on a chessboard the possibilities become astronomical. By this analogy God responds to an infinite range of possibilities. God takes into account even our wrong choices and, as Paul said, in everything "works for good with those who love him, who are called according to his purpose" (Rom 8:28). There is a guidance, perhaps even a certain amount of determinism, in this, for God is moving all things toward *some* meaningful goal. But the determinism is not a *particular* determinism. It is a *general* one. And we may even ask whether the *ultimate* goal has been set, for we are talking about God's personal direction of things. The goal itself is dependent on God's fitting real choices together so that they form some meaningful pattern. How the game turns out is decreed by the sum total of moves that have been made.

To allow for a greater measure of freedom, on the one hand, places a greater responsibility upon us, as the Scriptures teach. The range of possibilities at the inanimate level is very restricted, of course; consequently, one hardly talks about natural disasters such as earthquakes as "evils," certainly not as *moral* evils. These would have to occur as a result of freedom or contingency that God has built into the universe, but there could be little responsibility attached to them. At the animate level, however, both freedom and responsibility increase. Finally, at the human level these reach their peak. Human beings do not have unlimited freedom, but they have a vast amount; they are capable of using and controlling nature, animals, and even other persons. Thence they have responsibility commensurate with this freedom. They are responsible for their own life, for the life of their fellow human beings, and for the world in which they live.

Evil, therefore, is related to freedom. It is not something that exists in and of itself, a power equivalent to God, but the failure to accept responsibility for choosing the good or deliberate choice to the contrary. In other words, it is not merely something that I should not do; it is much more my failure to do what I should. When God grants me the capacity to participate in God's creative work and I fail to respond according to that capacity, I violate God's will. Is this not the rebuke that Jesus issued to the Pharisees? Pharisaism broke no rules, but it neglected things of greater importance. Jesus' rule was: Much is expected of one who has received much. Paul likewise spoke of a universal responsibility: "All things are yours; and you are Christ's; and Christ is God's" (1 Cor 3:22-23).

What this stewardship may entail in our day will be discussed in the next chapter. Meantime, I would point out that there is another consequence of understanding God as the chess master who responds to the complex of choices that we make. This understanding should alleviate persons of the onerous burden that, given only an either/or, they have made a wrong choice. Many live with such burdens of guilt, sometimes suffering severe mental disorders as a consequence. In this view, however, God is capable of using even erroneous choices to bring good out of evil. This does not mean certainly that all things will automatically turn out all right, so that we need not worry about what we do. Far from it. Some evils cannot be rectified in and of themselves. For example, the death of someone caused by criminal negligence is a tragedy that cannot be erased even by God. God has allowed freedom for evils of this type, and God will not violate human freedom. But this evil can produce a good in relation to another individual and set of circumstances. For example, it might generate a sense of responsibility in the guilty person or in the society that will save other lives.

The evolutionary process depends on negatives as well as on positives for its forward and upward progress. It has in it a substantial amount of trial and error. Some species die in order that stronger and more durable ones might live. In some such way God moves the whole panorama of events toward some meaningful end. God parlays the complex array of combinations in such a way that good ultimately will triumph as God becomes "all in all." The power of love is stronger than the power of evil.

This personalistic model of God is one that cannot be demonstrated by rational or empirical proofs. To be sure, you may find some support in the arguments from design, moral oughtness, ontology, etc. But these will help the person who is already predisposed to believe. In the final analysis, belief in God as personal reality, as the heavenly Parent involves bending the knees of our minds, recognizing that God is not the God of philosophers and the learned, but the God of Jesus Christ, your God and mine. God is found by the ways taught in the gospel, as Blaise Pascal said.

To believe in God is to gamble. It is better to gamble that God is, to cite Pascal's famous wager argument. For if I wager that God isn't and it turns out that God is, I have lost everything. If I wager that God is and it turns out that God isn't, I have lost nothing. But if I wager that God is and it turns out that God is, I have gained everything.

Chapter Three

Devotion in Our Activities

The preceding chapter dealt with the conceptual problem that underlies the other problems of devotion. The next step is to seek a solution to the problem posed by secular life-style, that is, how we conceptualize God fitting into the schedule of our activities. In a society dominated by religion, of course, this was not a serious issue, for a religious significance could be imposed upon the clock, the calendar, and all other matters of importance. In a secular society, however, it is a serious issue. Not only do secular forces, often indeterminate ones, regulate the *secular* clock, calendar, and other things but they even encroach upon those that are supposedly "religious." Gradually God and religion are "edged out." What can we do?

Secularization or Sacralization?

Instinctively, I think, most of us will respond with a defense of approaches hallowed by tradition. Some Roman Catholics, for example, have reached the saturation point regarding changes in the Mass that have occurred since Vatican II. They complain that rendering it in the vernacular and opening it to experimentation have desacralized it. "It no longer seems like a *religious* service." A number of these persons have felt strongly enough about the innovations to risk excommunication by meeting in unapproved enclaves to celebrate the Mass in the old style.

One can sympathize with this kind of reaction. Similar ones can be found among all religious groups. Change is frightening. And the accelerated rate of change in our day, depicted so vividly by Alvin Toffler, has psychological and physiological effects that encourage a reversion to routines in which we feel comfortable. It is not surprising to find a decided conservatism about religious practices among young executives who are forced to respond to continuous accelerated change in their jobs. The church offers one sanctuary against change—the same fixed hours of worship, the same hymns, the same Scriptures, the same promises, the same prayers.

Sympathy aside, however, the problem with the separation of sacred and secular is that it inevitably leads to the substitution of proximate for ultimate concerns. "Religious" objects and activities become ends in themselves to the neglect of weightier matters. William Golding has exposed this danger graphically in *The Spire*. An English rector yearned to erect the grandest spire in all of Christendom to the glory of God. His desire became an obsession. He threw his whole self into the project. But, alas, when he was ready to put the capstone in place, the spire shook, crumpled, and fell. Its foundation would not support it. The rector perished in the rubble.

This is a particular problem in America, for the form of secularization that we have experienced has caused religion to be individualized and interiorized. For many it is "a purely private affair." Protestants, in particular, have contested stoutly efforts to apply religious principles to social and political issues. The result is, as Reinhold Niebuhr puts it, "moral man and immoral society." When coupled with a powerful pragmatism fostered by our economic system, this has meant that the religious perspective has been relegated to an increasingly limited sector and the churches have become, as often as not, perpetuators and not correctors of social evils.

In reaction to the compartmentalization of religion, radical theology, as I said earlier, represented a wholesome if overzealous corrective. From Bonhöffer on, radical theologians urged the churches to "religionless Christianity." Exactly what Bonhöffer meant by this phrase, originally coined by Karl Barth, is not clear. To many of his followers, however, it meant the abandonment of religious institutions. The goal of Christians should be not isolation from the world but identification with it. Like Christ, we are called to be human. We are to be "the man for others." Religious activities create barriers. They make one conscious of our separation rather than our identification with our fellow human beings. Therefore, it is essential that the churches give up their lives in order that Christians may fulfill their purpose.

As Harvey Cox, who has represented a moderate form of radical theology, argued in *The Secular City*, Christians are not to resist secularization. They should welcome it, for it is bringing freedom from the occult forces that have held persons in thrall. The secular city is to be lauded for its chief features—mobility, anonymity, pragmatism, profanity—for these promise optimum conditions for liberation. The secularization process, the secular city, is, as it were, the Kingdom of God. Therefore, Christians should celebrate fully what is happening in the secular city. The task of the church can be described as the proclamation (*kerygma*) of this liberty, ministering (*diakonia*) to the diverse needs within the city, healing the fragmentation there (*koinonia*), and expelling its demons (exorcism).

The value of this thought lies in an authentic Biblical insight that it has laid hold of. Jesus certainly repudiated compartmentalization in religion. Thus did he rebuke those who said their prayers on street corners, who fasted ostentatiously, and who gave alms so that others might marvel at their piety (Matt 6:1 ff.). We are not to put on an act about our religious commitment. Moreover, Jesus manifested disdain for religious rules about the Sabbath, fasting, foods, and other things when these got in the way of true devotion to God. Likewise, he condemned the Pharisees for tithing even the trivia while neglecting matters of far greater consequence.

The question is, however, whether radical theology went too far both in what it approved and in what it denied. As to what it approved, I think there is legitimate reason to question whether the secular life-style is deserving of the praise heaped upon it by most radical theologians. True, the technological culture has humanized life. It has elevated Western persons' standard of living to unimagined plateaus and made available to them things that ancient persons scarcely dreamed of. Medical technology, for example, has lengthened our life span, eliminated dreaded diseases, and stayed the hand of death. Mechanical technology has eased the human burden of toil and increased the produce of the soil thirty, sixty, and a hundred fold. One could go on and on describing the incredible achievements.

Still, all are not blessings. For in every area in which it has humanized life, this technological civilization has equally dehumanized it. Accordingly, the raising of our standard of living within the urban setting is counterbalanced by massive problems of community breakdown, crime, use of drugs and alcohol, and so on. The saving of life by medical technology is counterbalanced by the destruction of life by bombs, gas, germ warfare, guns, and other weapons. The increasing of mobility and the lightening of labor by mechanical technology are counterbalanced by air, soil, and water pollution and wasteful consumption of resources, to the point of creating an energy crisis. The improving of production by agricultural technology is counterbalanced by the depletion of the soil and poisoning of wildlife and even of human beings themselves. One could extend the list of negatives.

It is becoming increasingly evident, too, that the benefits of the metropolis are benefits gleaned by the affluent. The highly praised mobility of the secular city, for instance, is something that the poor do not enjoy. The poor are trapped in ghettos, which deprives them of dignity and reduces them to a subhuman level.

So radical theology went too far in what it approved. As to what it denied, there are grounds for questioning whether, in its concern to end the sacred-secular dichotomy, radical theology did not level things out too much. To be sure, there should be no artificial religious distinctions between people, places, and objects. But is this the same as saying that all things, therefore, have the same significance for religion? Such a conclusion, I think, does not take properly into account our intentions. Granted that the Kingdom or rule of God is found within the city, ought one to equate everything that transpires there with the Kingdom of God? Surely the process of dehumanization is not to be seen as God's activity!

The theology that I argued for in the previous chapter would tend to suggest that we should think about our activity in terms of *degrees of sacralization*. This is quite a different thing from *spheres of sacred and secular*. It recognizes that, although *potentially* all things are under God's rule, *actually* they are not. The freedom of human beings, for instance, allows them to deny or even to resist God's *actual* rule. No person or thing is totally submissive and concordant with God's will. All vary by *degrees* in the conscious intention or effort they make to submit to and to agree with God's will. The higher the level of consciousness, the greater the degree of possible sacralization. Human beings, for example, can comprehend, submit, and agree voluntarily with the divine will to a greater degree than matter, which has a minimal consciousness, or plants and animals, which are also limited.

The Christian's and the church's mission within the secular city, therefore, is not merely to call attention to the Kingdom of God but to invite persons to participate in it. In other words, the church seeks to actualize the potential. For this reason, the concept of the City of God, which radical theology tossed aside rather hastily, seems to me to be still useful. It reminds us that the human city is always less than it can be, that God has a further purpose that we have not yet achieved, that we have no enduring city here (Heb 13:14). The church itself, of course, strives to offer a model of the city of God, never a perfect one, to be sure, but a reasonable facsimile is God's design—of what humanity can be as it submits to God's rule.

"Religious" activities, therefore, have a proper function so long as they are aimed at obtaining that surrender and acquiescence of will by which the degrees of sacralization are deepened. They *symbolize* what we intend in our activities. They are not the intention itself, our commitment to God, for that can be actualized only in what we are and do. They are *signs* of the intention or commitment. How fortunate that we so easily substitute the sign for the commitment and thus let the latter die there. Our aim is, as Paul says, to offer ourselves as living offerings to God— this is our "reasonable worship" that is "holy and acceptable" to God (Rom 12:1-2).

The Increase of Love of God and of Neighbor

If my contention is sound, all of our activity will have meaning, but some activities will have more meaning than others. Their significance will increase to the extent that they are brought consciously under God's rule. The fact that human beings possess a higher level of consciousness imposes on them a greater degree of responsibility to select purposeful activities. Within an activistic society, of course, selecting activities meaningfully is highly problematic, as I shall point out at the end of this chapter. Presently we need to look at some responsibilities that rest upon us as participants in God's creative activity.

For one, if the evolutionary perspective is correct, human beings have an awesome responsibility with reference to their own evolution. In *The Future of Man*, Teilhard set out three factors that would be necessary if we are to discharge this: (1) the conservation of knowledge, (2) the unification of humankind, and (3) the cooperation of science and religion. Unfortunately Teilhard was not a very practical man, and he did not wrestle with the immense problems that his proposals posed. The first is entirely possible, of course, for computers now store immense amounts of data. The larger problem today is to sort out and interpret the multifarious data. The other two conditions are obviously well beyond the foreseeable horizon. In some ways our technology brings us close together, for example, in terms of communication and transportation. But at the same time, if Charles Reich is right about "Consciousness III,"[17] it has increased our individualism. Furthermore, nationalism seems to be growing rather than waning. Though Teilhard was warmly received in the scientific community, that welcome has not been extended to many other church persons. The long-range prospects do not seem good either, despite occasional signs of a detente.

Religious influence is needed, but hopes of this should be realistic. The possible control of evolution by human science presents some frightening as well as promising prospects in cloning, genetic engineering, organ transplants, involuntary sterilization, and artificial insemination, among other things. Science and technology have not exhibited much conscience about their experiments and inventions, though a few scientists have tried. The chief hope, I suppose, barring the participation of theologians in high-level planning, is that the churches or religious groups may awaken the conscience of society to dangers.

A more realistic concern that should guide Christian activity is to participate with God in the overcoming of evil, not natural but personal and social evil. To distinguish between good and evil is not easy in our complex society. Changes are occurring so rapidly that moral decisions we now have to make do not touch base with older ethical systems. Moreover, as a consequence of our consumer orientation, it is easy to become convinced that "the end justifies the means." Advertising agencies and the mass media are enlisted to sell products. No one asks whether the products are good or bad (until a crusader like Ralph Nader appears on the scene). It is assumed that all products are good so long as anyone buys them. Radio and television saturate our minds with the necessity of purchasing their products. The end result of the whole system is that values are thrown into confusion. Proximates are put in the place of ultimates and ultimates are discarded entirely.

One hesitates to speak of an example, but the complex Watergate affair illustrates graphically our difficulty. The principals all appear to be persons of high *individual* moral propriety. However, they became so convinced that the welfare of the nation was tied up with the reelection of the President that they lost all sense of *social* moral propriety. Bugging, wiretapping, breaking into opponents' campaign headquarters, solicitation of illegal political donations, surveillance, defamation of character—nothing was too much to be justified by the major goal. The former head of the White House staff, H. R. Haldeman, epitomized the rationale with a note scribbled across a memo in March of 1970: "I will approve whatever will work—am concerned with results—not methods."

One of the more stimulating responses to the breakdown of moral systems is "situation ethics." Situation ethics tried to establish the biblical concept of *agape*-love as a firm base for meeting new moral situations. For a person who has a deep understanding of *agape* and has developed skill as a result of having applied it in numerous cases, this principle probably provides a fairly reliable guide for behavior. Unfortunately, most persons lack the required understanding and skill, and it is not surprising to see youths as well as adults reverting to Puritanistic ethical codes that will offer more specific guidance and will free them from the burden of making real choices.

Some ethical system that would fit midway between the older codes and situation ethics would seem advisable. The absence of a more carefully structured system all too often lets pragmatic interests dominate. We are clever at justifying and rationalizing what we decide to do.

The major concern that should guide our activity is "the increase of love of God and of neighbor," H. Richard Niebuhr's definition of the purpose of the church and its ministry.[18] Love of God and love of neighbor are, after all, the two great commandments laid down by Jesus (Mark 12:28-33). And love is the *sine qua non* of discipleship (John 13:34-35; 1 Cor 13).

Our toughest challenge today is probably *to increase love of God*. Modern human "God-consciousness," as I remarked earlier, has atrophied. Until Western society restores some balance between the rational and the intuitive, human beings will have difficulty experiencing transcendence and returning love to the transcendent.

The increase of love of God is partially an apologetic challenge, partially an educational challenge, but essentially a demonstrative challenge. Love is something that is not easily defended or explained in theory, for it is not a tangible entity. Furthermore, it is not the kind of experience that is subject to rational analysis and therefore taught like logic. This is why in the scriptures one finds no rational arguments for God's existence. Rather, God is presented as the God who acts. We experience God as redeeming love. In the Old Testament, Israel knew God's mercy, *hesed*, through the exodus and the wilderness wanderings. It was in Jesus of Nazareth, Israel's Messiah, that God's love was demonstrated as never before, however. This demonstration almost certainly formed the backdrop for the Christian understanding of the word *agape*, God's love given freely and without strings attached.

If God, then, manifests love in act, so also do we bear witness to it. Lin Yutang has given powerful confirmation of this in his spiritual autobiography, *From Pagan to Christian*. Lin Yutang was brought up in a Christian home but turned away from it in his teens because he could not accept some traditional doctrines. He became a Buddhist, a Taoist, and a Confucianist, which one may be at the same time. Later on, however, he returned to the Christian fold. The reason: on shipboard he met a Christian woman who exuded the warmth and kindness that should stem from Christian love. Lin Yutang's comment about this was, "This formula works as no doctrine works."[19] In the fourth century C.E. the Emperor Julian, seeking to restore paganism, paid Christianity the high compliment of imitating its charities. His letter to a pagan priest charged with effecting the revival in Galatia laid bare his reasoning. The reason that "atheism" (Christian belief in one God) was increasing was that, whereas the Jews took care of their own and the Gentiles took care of nobody, the "Galileans" (Christians) took care of everybody. So everyone was turning Christian.

The increase of love of neighbor will also be achieved with difficulty in Western society today, for the secular city has also caused our sensitivity to our fellow human beings to atrophy. The loss of the sense of the personal is not simply a loss suffered by the individual; it is a social loss as well. Who in America does not remember the name Kitty Genovese, the young woman stabbed to death while forty people stood by without turning a hand? Twice she broke away from her assailant. Three times she cried out for help. But no one wanted to get involved. Less well known but equally revealing was the mugging of a prominent New York City lawyer by two youths while a hundred people watched. The lawyer was beaten, his clothing was torn, his glasses were broken, but no one came to his aid. Afterward a reporter asked him, "How did you feel with those people standing by and refusing to help?" His reply was, "Well, that's New York." It is—New York, Chicago, St. Louis, Los Angeles, San Francisco—the whole mega-mess.

Without a radical change in the character of the secular city we have limited chances for the increase of love of God and of neighbor. This is not a book about the mission of the churches, organized communities of

Christians, but they obviously will carry the main portion of the load. They may exert pressure toward changes in urban patterns or seek to set up experimental models in human community on a smaller scale. In addition, Christian individuals may influence changes in unjust and amoral or immoral social structures through such groups as Common Cause, the Center for the Study of Democratic Institutions, or Ralph Nader Associates. Instead of lapsing into eschatological pessimism, we have to trust God's providence and exert as much influence as possible toward the right kind of change.

The individual Christian and groups of Christians will seek especially to exemplify love through action. Christian charity should not be based on evangelistic motives. Rather, both evangelism and charity should build on the motive of selfless love.

The word "love" is bandied about so much today that it has lost much of its true significance. To be sure, even perverse expressions of it may represent a fragment of true love, and one can but welcome all of these, whether the protesters' "Make love, not war" or the popular song's "Love makes the world go round." *Agape*-love encompasses all other kinds of love. But it should be distinguished from them in several ways: First, we are speaking here of God's love in us that flows out toward the other. Its source is not in ourselves but in God, so it is inexhaustible. It never gives up. As such, secondly, *agape* loves not on account of the others' attractiveness or merit but because that is its nature. It loves without expectation of return. Thirdly, *agape* loves the imperfect, the unlovable, because the other is a person, and does not try to fit that person into one's own mold. Fourthly, *agape* loves in particular. Indeed, here is where the real test comes. It is easy to say, "I love everybody" or "I love the universe." It is not easy to say, "I love Joe Doaks—freckles, big nose, alcoholism, swearing habits, and all."

This writer had an awakening to this truth when he was eleven or twelve years old. It was the first time he had played with a black boy his own age. One day it dawned on him that Tom was different from every other black person. He *was* a person, Tom. Until then, all black people were "black people"—nameless, faceless members of a race. Is this not really the crux of racism of all kinds—its impersonalism? People are "typed" and categorized: Chinks, wops, Dagos, Polacks, Japs, gringos, half-breeds, etc.

Christian history has produced some remarkable examples of this kind of love. There is no time to give a roll call of the saints. Hardly any surpassed Margaret Fell, the noble widow of a British magistrate who became the wife of George Fox. She exemplifies, it seems to me, both of the Christian ministries to our fellow human beings. Her story has been beautifully related in Jan De Hartog's *The Peaceable Kingdom.* Sometime after her conversion to the Friends movement through a meeting with the magnetic Fox, she visited an English prison where small children were kept. What she saw caused her to retch. Small children were confined in the lowest part of the prison, below hardened criminals, in dark, dank, rat-infested, lousy, unsanitary, stinking cells. They slept on dirty straw. The lady of noble demeanor and upbringing stayed, but she sent her maid to fetch cleaning utensils, clothing, food, and other things. She slept on straw amid filth, lice, rats, and children. Gradually, by love, she gained the children's confidence. But one small boy, condemned to be hanged as a murderer, would not let down his defenses. Eventually, however, love prevailed. She could not save his life, but she was able to ease the pain of his death.

If there is a way to increase love of God and of neighbor, it will be the way of Margaret Fell.

Activity and Contemplation

For most of us, the chief interest attaches to our everyday activities. In what way may our jobs, our household chores, our child-rearing tasks, and the plethora of other activities relate to our devotion? May they be related to God's will for our lives and contribute to God's ultimate purposes?

Teilhard de Chardin responded to these questions brilliantly in a letter to an industrialist friend in 1930. The friend wanted to know how the success of a commercial enterprise had anything to do with moral progress. Teilhard replied:

> . . . since everything holds together in a world which is on the way to unification, the spiritual success of the universe is bound up with the correct functioning of every zone of that universe and particularly with the release of every possible energy in it. Because your undertaking—which I take to be perfectly legitimate—is going well, a little

more health is being spread in the human mass, and in consequence a little more liberty to act, to think, and to love. Whatever we do we can and must do it with the strengthening and broadening consciousness of working, individually, to achieve a result which (even as a tangible reality) is required, at least indirectly, by the body of Christ. As you say yourself, to the value of the work done is added the value of the actual doing, which by its fidelity creates in us the personality expected of us by Christ. Our own soul—in itself and in its being at the heart of the universe—is the first of the tasks calling for our efforts. Because you are doing the best you can (even though you may sometimes fail), you are forming your own self within the world, and you are helping the world to form itself around you. How, then, could you fail from time to time to feel overcome by the boundless joy of creation?[20]

All activities, then, *may* express our commitment to God and God may use them in some way for the achievement of some ultimate purpose.

The Christian concern, however, it should be clear by now, is not merely activity but purposeful activity.

Once again, I fear, our modern life-style does not encourage purposeful activity. Far from it. It is characterized itself, rather, by activity for activity's sake, motion without direction, expenditure of time without profit.

The problem is not too many activities, although that is true for many, but too many *fruitless* activities. The result is that many feel dissatisfied with what they are doing. A recent survey of 2,821 business men and women by the American Management Association showed that nearly half have changed or considered changing occupational fields and a third believe they would have greater personal satisfaction or reward in another career. Forty percent of middle managers and fifty-two percent of supervisory managers stated that their work was unsatisfying.[21]

It is entirely possible that a vast shift in the general economic and labor picture could occur if enough persons refused to take positions that demanded too much of them physically or emotionally and compromised them morally. Many youths have been resisting the values and activities of their parents. Occasionally one hears of a person of middle age who makes a radical shift in occupation—say from a banker to a cab driver—in order to obtain satisfaction instead of financial reward. Some years ago, after I preached a sermon on Christian contentment, a young man related to me his decision to return to his hometown and take a job at lesser pay for which he had training and interest but which he had turned down for a higher-paying job five years before.

Still, the success motive is a powerful one. Where will those who feel dissatisfied with their activities find this more powerful motive to reorder activities so as to arrange in proper order proximate and ultimate concerns?

The study mentioned above listed in order of importance for job changes (1) "enhanced occupational status and authority" (898), (2) "salary considerations" (729), (3) "opportunity to spend more time with family" (306), and (4) "opportunity to reduce tension and health hazards" (260). There is little here to show cause for a shift to more meaningful activities. Many persons can pinpoint their frustration rationally, but knowing the problem is not enough.

The place to begin, I believe, is with contemplation. Until we begin to rediscover ourselves in relationship to the Self, God, to restore our relation to the ground of being, there is little hope that we can reassess our activities and begin to pour meaning into them. Jesus' counsel may be still applicable to our situation: "Seek first the kingdom (of God) and God's okaying of you, and all these things will fall into place" (Matt 6:33, my paraphrase). First priority must be given to the "one thing needful," or, better, the One who is needful, and then one may begin to see what should be done about activities.

The critical challenge is to gain perspective with reference to our activities and then to rearrange our lives in line with this new perspective. Because cultural patterns impose themselves so powerfully, it is difficult to gain such perspective until the Other breaks through and penetrates to the deeper levels of our consciousness. Is this not what happens to the prophet, the horizonal person?

It will be helpful to illustrate this "breakthrough" with a biographical example, Francis of Assisi.

Francis was the son of a wealthy merchant of Assisi, Peter Bernardone. For the first twenty years of his life he lived like other sons of affluence in his city. He did not notice the poverty of the masses that was a consequence of urbanization. All around him were jobless beggars, the unskilled who had left the farm for the freedom of the city but who could not do the crafts that would have brought employment. He enjoyed the parties thrown by wealthy friends, and he too gave parties. When the city of Assisi mounted a campaign against the neighboring city of Perugia, like any other utiful twenty-year-old son of Assisi, Francis donned his fine armor, mounted his powerful war-horse, and went to battle. Why Assisians ever went to battle against Perugia is a mystery, for Perugia was a virtually impregnable fortress, while Assisi was highly vulnerable to attack. But Francis did not ask why. He just went.

The campaign against Perugia evidently began a fateful change in Francis' life, though the facts are shrouded in legend. Before he ever struck a blow, he was captured and spent a year in prison. When he was released and returned to Assisi, people noticed a change. Francis was no longer a "devil may care" youth. He was not "the life of the parties." He had become moody. He sought solitude. Then he began to do strange things, but in what sequence it is difficult to say.

When Assisi mounted another military campaign, he, like others, was grandly outfitted. As he was getting ready to mount his horse, however, he spied a poor foot soldier in tatters and proceeded to give armor, horse, and all the rest to him and to set off alone for the open fields.

Another time, as he rode his horse, he saw a leper and heard him cry out in the way required by law when he approached another person. As on many another occasion, he reined his horse to one side of the path and spurred him past the wretched creature. But hardly had Francis gotten past before he reined up, dismounted, raced back and embraced and kissed the leper.

Another day, he took some cloth from his father's store, sold it, and took the proceeds to a local priest. The priest refused it, knowing that Peter Bernardone had not sent it. But when he handed it back, Francis grabbed the bag and hurled it down upon a window seat in the church. Again Francis went away. This was the last straw. One day, Peter Bernardone accosted Francis in the street. He upbraided him. "All that you have, I gave you. The clothes on your back—everything." Thereupon Francis proceeded to strip himself naked and hurl his clothes in a pile at his father's feet. He would have gone away stark naked except for the kindness of the bishop, who put his own robe around him.

Francis had become the apostle of poverty.

What caused it? The whole confluence of events perhaps. But perhaps something more. For in these events Francis had become a man of contemplation, of prayer, of solitude. Could it be that God broke through the outer shell to the inner person in contemplation?

To be a contemplative Christian will not necessitate becoming a monk, even if monasteries have been the traditional home of contemplatives. As Thomas Merton, a Trappist monk put it, "It is sufficient to be a child of God, a human person."[22] What is necessary is solitude. The question is, how will we find solitude in the beehive that the secular city is? Is a contemplative style of life possible at all today in the context of a secular style of life?

Chapter Four

The Contemplative Style

A sound that has echoed through this entire volume is the necessity of contemplation, not contemplation merely as another activity but as a style of Christian life. Unfortunately contemplation does not come easily in our context for, if there is anything that is *not* characteristic of us, it is withdrawal, solitude, and the devotional regimen that has characterized contemplation in the past. Indeed, monasteries, which fostered the contemplative style, have not been more seriously threatened since the Middle Ages. Monks like Thomas Merton have had to wrestle seriously with the question of "contemplation in a world of action," the title of one of his posthumous works. Merton's conclusion seems to have been that monks still had a vocation even if the institution should die.[23] Their vocation would be to witness to others by their lives concerning the monastic contemplative quest—the discovery of the ground of being, wisdom, truth, being itself, God. Others could also learn contemplation, and monks could teach them.

Contemplation means prayer or, better stated, the life of prayer. Prayer is something the churches have not taught well, judging by current signs. Many are turning elsewhere to get instruction—to Eastern religions (Buddhism, Hinduism, Taoism), to the popular teacher of transcendental meditation, the Maharishi Mahesh Yogi, to para-Christian cults, and so on. A discussion of prayer, therefore, will not prove superfluous. It is here, I think, that we reach the center of the life of devotion, for it is prayer that should integrate the Christian's existence in the world. In an encounter with God in prayer, at the center, we should discover our authentic personhood. Here we should be primed for meaningful existence within the world. Here we should find our activity redirected and consecrated to the purposes of God.

My discussion will revolve around three questions. First, Why pray? Second, What is prayer? Third, What does prayer do? That this is the correct order for the questions will become evident as we proceed.

Why Pray?

The primary and fundamental question is: Why pray? The answers to this question today go in three different directions.

In practice, many persons pray *for what they get out of it*. In short, they have a pragmatic interest in the exercise. This, at any rate, is a factor underlying the interest that many express in transcendental meditation. And, according to a study by Harvard psychologists Herbert Benson and R. Keith Wallace, meditators will not be disappointed. The Benson-Wallace study has shown physiological changes during meditation: (1) decreased oxygen consumption, heart rate, and metabolic rates; (2) increased electrical resistance of the skin; (3) heightened intensity of alpha brain waves; and (4) reduced production of lactic acid. Together these phenomena probably signify relaxation of tension and reduction of anxiety.

A promoter of the Maharishi's teaching in Kentucky, Richard Hill, envisioned immense social possibilities in meditation. On the social level TM might, by retooling the nervous system, make people happier, more content and fulfilled, and it may reduce crime, injustice, poverty, disease, drug abuse, and even general boredom. If it caught on like polio vaccine or pizza, Hill has observed wryly, it might take the country in ten years.[24]

One difficulty with this rationale is that, like the pragmatic approach to other things, it can be dispensed with when something better comes along. And, in the scientific and technological era in which we live, something better always seems to be coming along. Thus, whereas medieval persons prayed when they had a headache, now we take an aspirin tablet. Or whereas they had the priest pray and anoint their heads with oil, now we go to an M.D. Increasingly, prayer is edged out when a simpler and less demanding practical solution comes along.

A more serious difficulty is that this rationale turns God into an accommodating heavenly bellhop. If we need something, we ring the desk and God hurries along with our order. The rest of the time we can do without God. God is edged out farther and farther to the periphery of life as we become more confident of our self-sufficiency. Whether in reality or in imagination, we presume to have "come of age," as Bonhöffer put it, able to get along without a "God-hypothesis."

In reaction to this abuse of prayer and in recognition of the potential put in human hands by scientific knowledge, a number of persons, both in and outside the church, have asked, *"Why pray, indeed?"* Not all representatives would speak this way, to be sure, but radical theology took this direction. God, if there is a God, is in the world, in the secular city, in the activities of human beings. One's devotion, therefore, should take the form of activity. Whatever one does is prayer. In a conference on prayer in which I participated I heard a seminary student articulate this view rather bluntly. He became increasingly agitated over all the prayer talk. Suddenly he blurted out: "I don't see why we are wasting our time with all this talk about prayer. Everything I do is a prayer. When I kiss my wife—that's a prayer! When I take out the garbage—that's a prayer!"

A partial critique of this view has already been given in my insistence that activity that is not based on contemplation, though well intentioned, often becomes purposeless. This is, as Merton insisted, a deeply rooted problem of Western society, activity for activity's sake, which becomes activity without fruit and even destructive of human welfare.

But there's another problem, too. This attitude reduces our activities to one level. It pays too little attention to intention behind activities. To state the reply facetiously, should one not distinguish between kissing his wife and taking out the garbage? I am not sure I agree even with Teilhard—though I agree with him in many particulars—when he says in a prayer that "no one lifts his little finger to do the smallest task unless moved, however obscurely, by the conviction that he is contributing infinitesimally (at least indirectly) to the building of something definitive —that is to say, to your work, my God."[25] Does this allow sufficient room to think about intended evil, the misdirecting of human effort? I think not. However much our activities may contribute to God's ultimate purpose for our universe, there is value in offering these consciously and intentionally to God.

My own answer to the question, therefore, is: We pray *because we believe that God, as the heavenly Father, is as the ultimate personal reality in the universe.* This rationale, I believe, suits both the scriptures and the theological model that we have established.

We do not address God, "Oh, you great whatchamacallit." God is our heavenly Parent. Indeed, Jesus himself used the very intimate Aramaic word *Abba.* Joachim Jeremias has pointed out[26] that this word corresponds to the American word "daddy." He has illustrated this by relating a personal experience with current usage. When he dismounted the ramp of a plane in an Arab nation once, a young boy raced toward the plane to meet his father, crying out, *"Abba! Abba! Abba!"* So we approach God, the Father, "with boldness" (Eph 3:12; 1 Tim 3:13; Heb 4:16).

Such a personal conception suits our understanding of God as the divine love that fills the universe and moves it forward toward some meaningful goal. To use the striking phrase in 1 John 4:8, "God is love." Prayer, therefore, is motivated by love, which seeks naturally and spontaneously to interact with what it has made. Our love responds to God's love that is always beaming on us. Is it not as Augustine said in his *Confessions*? We wish to praise God. God arouses us to praise: "For you have made us for yourself, and our heart is restless until it rests in you."[27] The personal seeks the personal. The "I" seeks that "Thou." The "Lover" seeks the "beloved." Communion of person with person is an urgent necessity that nothing else in nature or in the pseudo nature of technology can supplant.

What is Prayer?

In giving this rationale for prayer, what prayer is has already become clear. But there are so many misconceptions or superficial conceptions of prayer abroad that we need to look at its meaning in some depth.

It will be helpful, I think, to point out that prayer is not something one says, words—perhaps not even something one does, an activity. Prayer may use words and it may involve activity, but these are too restrictive for communion between a person and God at the intimate level that the Bible presupposes for prayer. Paul spoke of "groanings that cannot be uttered" (Rom 8:26), "sighs too deep for words" that the Spirit of God must convey to God on our behalf. Words and activities only get us under way in prayer. Prayer itself represents the deepest, most heartfelt, most agonizing concerns of our inner selves. Perhaps it is essentially what Paul Tillich calls faith, "ultimate concern."

If prayer, in its essence, raises up to God our inarticulable concerns or desires, then we should focus our attention first upon our personal character. Our real concern should be not to learn how to frame verbal images better but to learn how to go beyond them in respect of pure desires and concerns of the heart. In short, we should seek "purity of heart." Thus will our "sighs" and "groanings" rise like incense to God's throne. The saints of Christian history attest that the purer our lives become in love, the more intimate will be our communion with God. The more the false and corrupting thoughts and desires drop away, the more we can convey to God of our intercessions for our fellows.

The developmental process of the Christian, that, incidentally, correlates well with modern psychology, seems to me to be well described in Bernard of Clairvaux's famous sermon "On the Love of God." The first is *love of self for self's sake*. Bernard wisely pointed out that everyone must *begin* there. We cannot love others unless we first love ourselves. Thus Jesus commanded, "You shall love your neighbor as *yourself*" (Matt 19:19, italics added). To put the same insight in Thomas Harris' language, unless I can say, "I'm okay," I will find it difficult to say, "You're okay." If I have a low self-esteem, I will have a low esteem for others too.

The second stage is *love of God for self's sake*, because God does what we want. This is a highly utilitarian approach to religion but, alas, one that many Christians possess. We love God so long as God is useful. But if God lets us down in sickness or in a crisis of life, we are done with God. How many, when a prayer for a loved one does not turn out as they decreed, avow: "I'll never pray again. I don't believe there is a God. If God exists, God is cruel and unjust"?

It is possible to go beyond this, therefore. The third stage is *love of God for God's sake* because God is eminently worthy of our love. We love God for creation, for redemption, for providence. In all circumstances we trust God because God has shown trustworthiness. As Bernard noted, this usually happens in times of crisis.

To many this might seem to be the highest possible stage of our growth in love. Bernard, however, takes us one step farther, to *love of self for God's sake*. At first glance he seems to have turned full circle to an egocentric love again. But he has not. Love of self for God's sake means total surrender, putting our lives at God's disposal for the working out of God's purposes. One cannot do more. Here is Jesus' prayer in Gethsemane—"Not my will, but thine."

To look more specifically at the process by which this communion might occur, I would speak of it, for the sake of memory, in terms of three turnings.

First, it is a *turning on*. If God is, as we have said earlier, the love that fills all things, holds them together, and directs them toward some meaningful end, then it should be possible to discern God's presence within the natural order as well as within ourselves. Is this not what the psalmist bore witness to when he declared, "The heavens are telling the glory of God; and the firmament proclaims his handiwork" (Ps 19:1)? Or the hymnist (Maltbie D. Babcock) when he sang, "This is my Father's world,/And to my list'ning ears,/All nature sings, and round me rings/The music of the spheres"? Or Robert Browning with his perhaps too optimistic cry in "Pippa Passes": "The hillside's dew-pearled;/The lark's on the wing;/The snail's on the thorn: God's in his heaven—/All's right with the world"?

But in our experience of God through nature, modern technological civilization is causing us to stumble, for it has snatched away our contact with nature and substituted for it the pseudo nature of technology. Our artificial environment extols the handiwork of human beings, not the handiwork of God. And, despite the marvelous advantages that urban lifestyle brings, our detachment is creating something of a crisis, a crisis that may go deeper than the absence of trees, grass, flowers, soil, sun, moon, and stars.

Superficially this crisis created by an artificial environment seems to be taken care of in our mobile society by flight from the city back to nature: living in the country and commuting to work daily or weekly, moving to small towns to take jobs at lower salaries, genteel farming, trekking to national parks or the mountains, camping, and hiking. Even these, it should be noted, are options for people of means and not for the poor; the poor do not have and cannot afford this kind of mobility. But even for the affluent, if the problem has a deeper root in a severance of human beings from their ground of being, as the nature crisis implies, then these solutions will not suffice. Growing dependence upon drugs, alcohol, and other artificial remedies do, in fact, confirm that casual contacts with nature are not sufficing. By nature, human beings require rootage in the ground of being—if you please, in God.

A Parisian psychiatrist, Pierre A. Bensoussan, has blamed the current alcohol and drug crisis in Western society on our artificial life-style. He questions whether modern persons are capable of adapting biologically as fast as changes are occurring in their environment. More and more people feel that they have nothing exciting to look forward to. Dr. Bensoussan insists that the solution lies in providing "spiritual activity," not necessarily that supplied by some religious groups but "something of value to do in our span of life in this world."[28]

Those who wish to see God in God's handiwork, therefore, must look elsewhere. One other source, surely, even within the seething metropolis, is in the face of our neighbor. We are, after all, the crown of God's creative work, that part that has the capacity for sharing in creation, and the one that bears the stamp of God's own nature. The anonymity of the secular city is, unquestionably, a problem, *pace* Harvey Cox, unless we find ways to experience community at a deeper level than we are now doing. But the church can help in this. And, despite what might be said in criticism of it, even the institutional church of today provides a locus for finding this community. We do, however, need to be searching for other forms of the church. No question is perhaps as urgent as the question: Where is the church? We will not necessarily see it under its customary forms. Nor will we find an orthodox constituency. What we will need to look for, above all, are signs of the divine love breaking through to create a bond of brotherhood and community.

Secondly, prayer is *a turning in*. It is meditation.

The immense interest in meditation, despite its being done for the wrong reasons, is much to be welcomed. Christian meditation, however, differs significantly from other types in its focus on scriptures. TM, one or another form of Yoga, the psychologist's introspection, or Zen meditation attempt to get meditators to focus upon something external, such as a mantra. Although these may be useful to us as a preparation for meditation, they should not be considered prayer itself.

Why focus on scriptures? The object is to have formed in us "the mind of Christ," as Paul says in Philippians 2:5. It is not by chance that Christian meditation has relied heavily on the Gospels. Although all of scriptures can direct us in some ways to Christ, it is the Gospels that bear the most direct witness to him. They lead us to *the* Teacher par excellence. Above all, we need to open minds and hearts to let the Risen Christ invade and transform our minds and hearts. We pray as Augustine did in his *Soliloquies* after his conversion: "Teach me to know myself. Teach me to know Thee."[29]

Conceptually it is helpful to remember that God, as personal being, is present everywhere. The medieval mystics used to say, "God is He whose center is everywhere, whose circumference is nowhere." This means that God's center of consciousness, God's reality, is in my center of consciousness. God is waiting there for me to open the door of my inner self. Because God has created us free, God does not violate this inner chamber. The opening has to be voluntary. How well Michel Quoist has expressed that in his prayer entitled "Lord, Deliver Me from Myself." In the final section God answers the agonized pleader:

> I have long been watching your closed shutters. Open
> them; my light will come in.
> I have long been standing at your locked door; open it;
> you will find me on the threshold.
> I am waiting for you, the others are waiting for you,
> But you must open,
> You must come out.
> Why choose to be a prisoner of yourself?
> You are free.
> It is not I who locked the door,
> It is not I who can open it.[30]

We hesitate to speak of our own experience, but the one who prays does experience presence, not always, but now and then. Bernard of Clairvaux spoke of this as the "comings" of the Word. He testified that these had occurred to him many times. He did not know when Christ came or left, but he sensed his presence. So one may find in George Fox, Brother Lawrence, John Wesley, John Woolman, and others a low-key but positive witness to the sense of transcendence that many of us may experience at another level and in various ways. At these other levels the experience may have to do also with a feeling of wholeness, with being at home in one's inner sanctuary, with being at peace in oneself, with reconciliation, and harmony and contentment.

Thirdly, prayer is *a turning over*, a surrender of one's life to God.

This appears to me to be the most distinctively Christian prayer. But we must not speak of surrender and submission in a glib and superficial way. Bushels of lip service are given to singing and saying, "I surrender all." Yet the deeper surrender that is associated with this kind of prayer is missed altogether. We are talking here about loving God with all our "heart, mind, soul, and strength"—with our total personalities. Such a submission as this could not allow us to harbor racism in our hearts, to be almost inextricably enmeshed in life-styles that wasted the spaceship earth's limited resources, to drive without feeling through dirty and rat-infested ghettos, to leave ecological concerns to political and legal solutions.

This, you see, returns us to what I argued about prayer earlier. In its essence, prayer has to do with the transparent life. It is, as James Montgomery's hymn says, "the soul's sincere desire, unuttered or expressed." Where a life has become increasingly refined in its love, it becomes itself a kind of prayer. One's activities take on new meaning. They, too, are purified. Thus by our expression of love through activities others may discern that we know God (1 John 4:7 ff.).

What Prayer Does

This brings us to our final question regarding prayer, i.e., what it does. Although I have insisted that pragmatic concerns do not provide a proper rationale for prayer, I would not want this to be interpreted as implying that prayer does nothing. It does do something. The major issue is whether it does something to and for us alone or more than that.

Surely none of us will have difficulty believing that prayer does something to the person who prays. The study of meditators cited earlier points to physiological effects that have implications for emotional well-being. It confirms, I think, the conclusion of meditators through the centuries, namely, the conclusion that contemplation is the path to peace, harmony, integration of self, wholeness, and so on. So it is not surprising to witness the growth of this practice in a society that manufactures the very opposite of these.

Many have found also that prayer is where intuitive understanding occurs. Contemplatives gain a vision. They glance beyond the horizon to see where God is directing human events. Prophets, surely, are persons of prayer. Though they may depend on reason to a certain point, a special blik carries them beyond this. Their insight comes to them as a Word of the Lord.

How we explain intuitions of this sort will depend upon our presuppositions or biases. Some would ascribe them to the workings of the human mind. While no one can doubt the marvels of humankind itself, those who believe in a transcendent personal might properly attribute them to an external objective source. God breaks through the human conscious and penetrates to the subconscious. It is this kind of external intrusion that offers hope that one might break out of the cultural prison in which human understanding is so easily incarcerated in order to perceive reality directly.

Our own era, few will doubt, needs horizonal persons, those who are not simply molded in the pattern of their own era but who can look beyond. Seeing beyond takes place when the enduring reality becomes manifest in our experience. Was it not this that impelled Francis of Assisi in an era of transition from an agrarian to an urban culture to renounce his family's affluent life-style and to identify with the poor—as he depicted this decision, marrying Lady Poverty? Was it not this that caused John Woolman, before the American Revolution, to limit his own business in order that he might have time to travel at his own expense all over the American colonies, entreating Quakers to free their slaves?

But we should ask, too, a harder question about prayer: Does our prayer, this communion with God in which we bring all our deepest concerns before God, perhaps contribute to the fulfillment of the divine purpose for humankind and for the creation? And—related to and dependent upon this question—should we pray for specific concerns?

Our answer to the first question depends upon our understanding of God and God's relation to the world. If God is, as God has traditionally been depicted, the immutable or unchangeable One who has fashioned a world that operates like a clock, then the answer is almost certainly negative. If the world processes move inexorably toward some predetermined goal, predestined to turn out thus and so, then prayer will contribute little to the final outcome. It may help you and me to become reconciled to the inevitable, but it will not have anything to do with God's ultimate direction of things.

If, however, we adopt the model of God proposed earlier, it may be possible to ascribe a genuine efficacy to prayer. The model that I have suggested is that of the chess master. In accordance with this model, God does not program the exact processes of the universe ahead of time, so that they will occur in exactly the way prescribed. Rather, God responds to the specific choices that we make, even wrong ones, and makes moves so as to direct events toward an ultimately fruitful, but not necessarily predetermined, conclusion. This, then, makes room for maximum human input.

Our question here is: Is *prayer* a part of the input? Does it have anything to contribute to God's decisions in response to our decisions?

Our activistic society has tried to teach us to say no to both questions. All that is real is activity, doing. Prayer is effective if, when you have prayed, you feel constrained to do something to effect what you prayed about. Thence, if you pray for a poor family and then go feed them, your prayer will have meant something. In and of itself, we seem to suspect, prayer does nothing.

Taking the model proposed above, I think we have a right to challenge this assumption. If God makes decisions, as the chess master, in response to mine, then, when I pray, could not my prayer add factors to the base for decision-making? Let us think of this specifically with reference to the concern that prompts my prayer. Does my agonizing outpouring of love energies in prayer add an element to the divine love that moves things forward toward a purposeful conclusion? For example, if I pray out of love for someone who is physically or emotionally ill, could not God add that to God's own love energies out of which healing could occur?

Such a conclusion seems to me to be further warranted in the light of the scriptures and personal experience. Paul, for instance, assured the Philippians that even hostile conditions would turn out for his safety "through your prayer, and the supply of the Spirit of Jesus Christ" during his Roman imprisonment (Phil 1:19). The letter of James represents a strong conviction that "the energetic prayer of a person who is intimate with God has great strength" (Jas 5:16, my paraphrase). Morton Kelsey, an Anglican minister who taught for a time at the University of Notre Dame, has assembled a strong argument from Scriptures, church history, and theology for what he prefers to call "sacramental healing."[31] If what he says is true, then prayer takes on much greater import than merely to influence the psyche of the person who prays. God may use it to effect God's own ultimate purpose for God's creation.

To express such a naive confidence about prayer brings us to the real crux: how to explain God's failure to come through on what appear to us to be legitimate petitions. I pray for the recovery of my sick friend, but she dies. Why? Was the prayer permissible and legitimate? Or, should I have prayed only in generalities?

To take the questions in reverse, I do not think one can pray in generalities if prayer represents our deepest concerns. Our lips may talk in generalities, but our hearts will be far from them. Our hearts will bring specifics before God that we cannot put into words—our "sighs" and "groans." So no one should think that we can pray in abstractions; these would not even echo our real prayer.

This means that my prayer for the friend who was ill was legitimate. Certainly it was unavoidable. I could no more stop it from breaking through to God than I could cease all concern. Further, God wills health and life, not sickness and death.

Then why, when I prayed for her to live, did she die? If God is good and wishes health for us, why did God not save her? God alone can give the immediate and specific reasons. In general, however, the answer lies in the self-limitations that God has accepted in order to build freedom into the universe. Presumably God could have created a perfect universe where all things moved with the precision of a clock. But God wishes a universe that reflects God's own personal nature. In love, therefore, God granted freedom. This freedom means suffering for God, but it is a part of love's nature to suffer gladly. Under the circumstances, in this partic- ular case, then, God could not put together all the conditioning factors, all the moves that have been made, in such a way as to save my friend. Given God's own decision to act as the chess master, God could not suddenly disregard all the other moves made in the game.

When we pray, therefore, we may pray specifically and yet be in keeping with God's nature if we pray open-endedly. Our real difficulty in making petitions and intercessions lies not in being specific but in trying to dictate what the answer must be. Jesus, after all, taught the disciples to pray for "daily bread." To wish to supply answers is natural to us, but it is at the same time an expression of our "littleness of faith," as Jesus stated it. Our loving petitions and intercessions require trust in God as the heavenly Father who is just as concerned about the creation as we are, or more so. Our petitions complement God's own loving con- cern, through which in everything God "works for good with those who love God, who are called according to God's purpose" (Rom 8:28). Is it too much to believe that sometimes our feeble outpouring of love in prayer, added to that of others and merged into God's boundless love, may supply the extra something that will "move mountains"?

There is a delightful illustration of my point in one of the Doctor Seuss books that so many parents read to their children, *Horton Hears a Who*. Horton, the elephant, heard a "Who" speaking to him in a red clover blossom. But none of his friends would believe him. They laughed. They ridiculed. They caged Horton. Then they had an eagle carry the blossom miles away and drop it in the midst of a whole field of red clover blossoms. But Horton, still believing, searched. He searched and searched until at last he found the red clover blossom in which he had heard a Who. To persuade his friends, he exhorted all the Whos of Whoville to make all the noise they could. The Whos shouted. They played their brass bands. But they weren't heard until the littlest Who was found and yelled out one little "Yopp." That did it. The Whos broke through and Whoville was saved.

Could it be that in prayer we offer that one little "Yopp"?

Chapter Five

The Simplification of Life

In our age the contemplative life-style will lead to the simplification of life.

Most people who live in the metropolis today are aware experientially of the complexity of life in a technocratic society. What is producing this complexity and the dangers latent in it has been brilliantly described by Alvin Toffler in his best-selling work, *Future Shock.*

Our society, says Toffler, is characterized by permanent transiency, novelty, and diversity. The only thing that is stable is change. Changes, due to technology, are occurring at a continually accelerated rate. This *rate* of change has implications that extend far beyond the *direction* of change. And, unless we become infinitely more adaptable and capable than ever before, we may lapse into a kind of physiological and psychological coma. Moreover, too many "future-shocked" individuals could produce a future-shocked society.

Future shock will manifest (should we say, is *manifesting*?) some of the same symptoms as combat fatigue or shell shock. First—confusion, disorientation, or distortion of reality. Next—signs of fatigue, anxiety, tenseness, or extreme irritability. Finally—apathy and emotional withdrawal. Individuals may respond to future shock in varied ways. *Emotionally*, they may react by blocking out reality, by specialism, by reversion to previously used but now outmoded adaptive routines, and by oversimplification. *Physically*, they may meet the challenge by "copping out" on drugs and artificial "trips," by violence, or by withdrawal.

A Primary Concern: Discovering the Center

The contemplative life-style, as I have depicted it, will coincide at many points with Toffler's proposals for averting future shock. At the broad social level he advocates "the conscious regulation of technological advance" and a "strategy of social futurism." At the individual level, which is our concern here, he urges the acquisition of "new principles for pacing and planning life" along with a new kind of future-oriented education. Periodically we should take stock of our own physical and psychological reactions to change and then adjust these reactions. We should build "personal stability zones," which will provide at the same time a radically different orientation to the future in anticipation of change. Those who have difficulty finding "personal stability zones" will require the help of others: situational groupings, crisis counseling, "half-way houses," enclaves of the past or of the future, and "global space pageants."

Our principles for pacing and planning life are, of course, religious ones. They originate in a commitment to the personal reality at the center of the universe, the "one thing needful," the Kingdom of Heaven. The crux in simplification is not merely changing the clock and calendar and life-style, for we will not do that without a more powerful inner motive. The crux lies, rather, in what the Quakers call "centering down," as Thomas R. Kelly says, "finding the holy Centre where the breath and stillness of Eternity are heavy upon us and we are wholly yielded to Him."[32]

From this Center other things will begin to fall into place—both our physical and psychological or spiritual reactions—it is hoped. Life will become simplified. We will develop a "sense of things that matter," as I would paraphrase Paul's prayer in Philippians 1:10.

On the one hand, we will see that many things that formerly had consequence now do not matter. The fact is, life-style as it now exists in the West is determined largely by external forces. The development of the mass media, particularly television, has altered the way we make selections and even the way we think about ourselves. Modern advertising has become adept at manipulating our subconscious desires from which our conscious choices derive. It appeals not merely to our rational selection, which in itself would not be bad, nor even to our sensory tastes, but to our psychological and emotional mechanisms. Thus, the real "he-man" will whiff the smoke of a certain brand of cigarette, the "man of distinction" will quaff a certain bourbon whiskey, and the person who craves companionship will "fly the friendly skies" of a certain airline.

To regain control of our values, then, will necessitate the discovery of an integrative center from which to establish a different kind of rapport with the world and the society of people around us. This discovery will assist us in the elimination of some activities and goods that we once counted essential.

On the other hand, a new constellation of priorities and values may begin to emerge. I take this to be the gist of Jesus' injunction, "Seek first the kingdom (of God) and God's okaying of you, and all these things (food, clothing, shelter) shall fall into place for you" (Matt 6:33, my paraphrase). To put this in Kierkegaard's words, this means "to will one thing." Once we have discovered the "one thing needful," we will not fret and worry about whether we have "enough." We will begin to discern things that are needful in their proper order. The reason we become anxious and fretful is that we substitute proximate for ultimate values. Matters of little real consequence take on "life or death" proportions. For many Americans the ultimate concern may be a football game, a basketball game, a baseball game. Just how deeply this penetrates to the point of being an ultimate surfaces periodically when an unruly, unhappy crowd waylays, maims, or even kills opposing players, coaches, or the referees or umpires in a game. For others the ultimate concern may be a political party, a candidate for office, a job, a bank account, a fine home, antique furnishings, and so on ad infinitum.

Once more the challenge is to "center down" and to determine from the Center the order of priorities.

Centering down may lead to vastly different types or degrees of simplification of life-style. The key issue is, I suppose, how far we wish to go in detachment from our modern technologic civilization. Will it be total renunciation for the life of a hermit or of a Diogenes? A few have been prepared to go that far even in our day. The trouble with this approach is that, with population growth and the development of technology, the world offers fewer and fewer places of complete isolation. Thomas Merton found even the Abbey of Gethsemane distracting and discouraging for a hermit, which he was from 1965 on. He was disappointed to learn that the Himalayas offered Buddist monks nothing quieter. Before his death he speculated that Alaska might provide "the very best place" for solitude,[33] but he was not confident. Not many, at any rate, will succeed as hermits; they never have.

Will simplification, then, lead to a communal monastic or semi-monastic retreat, Walden pond (Thoreau's or Skinner's), or some other refuge from dependence upon technology? These are options for some. The Anglican and Protestant churches have restored monasticism partially, and it is still a going, though flagging, concern within Roman Catholicism. The Children of God and a few other groups have developed semimonastic communal experiments. Unfortunately, the survival rate of communal groups in America has not been high over a long period of time. Two Shaker communities, dating from the late eighteenth century, survive, but they represent one exception among dozens of failures. The Amish Mennonites, who have both similarities to and dissimilarities with monasticism, have the most persistent record, but they are hard pressed to use technology to survive in a technological society. The Beachy Amish especially have gone modern; others give way little by little.

The other options would entail varying degrees of dependence upon technology and urban civilization and of detachment from present dependence. Will we, as many youths tried in the sixties, live in communes and share goods and resources in order to simplify and to stop waste? Will we, as many affluent people are doing, move to rural areas in order to enjoy most of the advantages of urban life-style without the disadvantages of the city itself? Or will we examine, as many are beginning to do, our current life-style in order to pare away some of its excesses both in consumption and in waste?

The first option has many admirable features. It coalesces with the early Christian experiment in Acts 2, and one would hope that many such experiments would succeed. Too many modern attempts, however, have been overly optimistic in assuming that each person would contribute according to ability in order that each might receive according to need. Selfish motives, unfortunately, intrude so powerfully that they undermine the workings of many communities and force the imposition of rigorous rules and restrictions. There is no clearer testimony to that than Robert Owen's ill-fated egalitarian experiment at New Harmony, Indiana, which after two years attracted so many freeloaders that the community had to be closed to all except intellectuals. If this kind of experiment is to succeed, it must begin with rules and be based upon a strong religious conviction.

The second option has a fundamentally selfish intent that, I should think, would not commend it unequivocally to the Christian. Whether it should pass for a simplification of life would depend upon the degree to which one would be willing to relinquish advantages of the city. It might be parasitic. It would not have much impact toward changing urban life-style itself.

The final option would seem to be that which most Christians will have to choose. They will, as the ancient Epistle to Diognetus said so well in the second or third century, live in the same cities with other persons, observe many of the same customs, but also manifest characteristics of their "confessedly strange citizenship." The real issue would seem to be how far we will go in being set over against a culture that gives evidence of so many features inimical to human well-being. Or, put the other way around, what might be a satisfactory Christian life-style in such a context? Without claiming definitive answers, let us look at the problem in two crucial areas—the use of time and the use of things.

The Proper Use of Time

The time problem today is not a problem of having time but of using time meaningfully. The fact is that technology has freed great blocks of time that we have not yet learned how to put to proper use. Whereas agrarian persons worked from "sunrise to sunset," dependent as they were on nature, urban persons are free to work around the clock. By virtue of technology, however, our hours of toil have been reduced to an average of thirty to forty hours a week, often scheduled as we wish.

Strangely, with the freeing of more time, the pace of life has speeded up. Nothing is more characteristic of our era, in fact, than a hectic, frenetic schedule. Large numbers of urban dwellers live as if each second may be the last, so that they must cram just one more activity into it. This desire to experience more and more in the allotted time has resulted in demands for faster and faster transportation. Within the past half century, cars have nearly doubled in average speed, planes have multiplied their speed rates many times over.

Most of these changes have occurred without our asking why, at least without our asking whether they would be beneficial. One immediate and highly visible consequence of the improvement of transportation to take care of increased speed demands has been a fuel crisis. More immediately germane to the issue we are dealing with here, however, is the impact the increased speed of our day is having upon us both physiologically and psychologically. Quite apart from the matter of ground and air accidents, we are learning that "Speed Kills!" The hectic pace of modern life, we are being told every day, is a factor in heart disease, emotional breakdown, alcoholism, drug addiction, and hundreds of other maladies. The physical and psychological apparatuses of many persons will not take the stress of this reckless pace.

Survival, therefore, depends upon simplification of schedule. The clearing of a cluttered calendar is only one aspect of the problem. Here is where from the Center we must ask ourselves some hard questions about the legitimacy of our activities.

The first question that one should ask is: Why am I doing this?

One has to be wary here, for we will find ourselves rationalizing the necessity of every activity in our calendars. "I am doing this because I just have to." Persons who pride themselves on selfless service to others will say, "I am doing this because my employer, my church, my friend, needs me."

In fact, most persons in the middle and upper income brackets are addicts of work. They suffer from what Wayne E. Oates has called "workaholism."[34] Perhaps they started in the lower income and lower cultural bracket. They got in the habit of working long hours. Gradually they find themselves without a taste for anything except work. They feel that they are shirking duty when they take time off for relaxation, for a vacation, for family fun. Not until illness, family problems, or other things strike do they realize that life offers other options. And the cure is as painful and torturous as that for other addictions—alcohol, drugs, smoking.

This addiction is a social problem, too. The "work ethic" has been built into the fabric of American life-style, beginning in colonial times. We do not honor the poor, as the Old and New Testaments do. Rather, we tend to look down upon them as failures in life. Had they applied themselves more diligently, they would not be where they are. The hero of America has been Horatio Alger, the man who pulls himself up by his own bootstraps, the enterprising man.

In a day when technology was not as developed as it is now, this penchant for work was doubtless a healthy thing. With the machine replacing or alleviating human labor, however, there is good cause to raise further questions. At a deeper level, we may ask, have we become so habituated to work while neglecting the development of our personal selves until we are afraid to stop working lest we find nothing to fill the work void? Stated another way, is our activism a cover-up for doubts about the reality of our selfhood? Or is it the construction of a false ego?

And is this not producing a Scrooge life existence that can find nothing but drudgery in life?

If these questions are pointing in the right direction, our centering down will cause a reassessment of our schedules in terms of meaning. The fact is that, upon this kind of examination, many activities in which one engages may prove relatively meaningless. Thirty years ago, to draw on a personal example, I was so busy I did not have time for exercise. I had to rush to and from work by car. To be sure that my family had transportation too, I had to buy an extra car. Three lengthy stays in England, however, incited my interest in walking. When I returned to the United States, I determined to walk more. In 1970 I began walking at least one way from my home to the seminary each day, a distance of three miles. The walk took about forty-five minutes. Once I could not have afforded the time, but now I am convinced that I could not have made better expenditure. My health improved. I am less irritable, more relaxed. I thought more clearly. I had opportunity for wholesome meditation, for, despite the traffic, a walk is in itself meditative.

From the Center, we will scrutinize our whole calendar. Is this activity meaningful? Have I spread myself out so thin that what I am doing means nothing either to me or to those whom I profess to serve? Most persons will be surprised at how much time may be freed in this way and how much new meaning can be poured into other activities. We may find that we control our schedules rather than being controlled by them.

It may be, too, that here lies the solution to the schedule problem of symbolic devotion. Although I do not believe that it will be possible, or desirable, for us to return to a medieval calendar of prayer five or six times a day, does the real problem lie in lack of time or in failure to take time? If the problem lies in the latter, then persons who are serious about their Christian calling will develop a disciplined schedule of meditation. This schedule may be, as mine is, brief interludes fitted into the work schedule many times during the day. Many short meditative periods are probably more effective than one or two long ones, but some persons may prefer long, sustained periods of meditation as they grow in discipline.

If there is not a real problem of time, moreover, the Christian may take longer periods for retreats and more meaningful recreations. All too often, even retreats become filled with activities, indicating again our fear of being still and seeking the Center.

The critical issue is whether we will control our schedules or our schedules control us. Nothing in modern, so called "secular" society restricts our calendars any more than in any other era. Indeed, our technological advances have freed time. But we have not made a corresponding effort to use meaningfully the time that has been freed. Instead, we have cluttered our calendars with fruitless activities that betray a deeper need and quest. The crises of the moment may cause us to seek a new list of priorities in our activities by which to recover the meaning of our efforts.

The Proper Use of Things

The need to learn how to use time meaningfully is matched or perhaps exceeded by a need to learn how to use *things* properly and meaningfully. Indeed, it is dependent upon doing so, for much of our abuse of time is a result of our quest for things. Simplification will mean here learning what is sufficient, being content with enough, not requiring more and more. In order for us to get started properly, it may at first require renunciation of things, somewhat like the monastic *contemptus mundi.* But it will not stop with that. The Christian's contentment will redound to the benefit of others. As Gerhard Kittel[35] has observed regarding 2 Corinthians 9:8: "Enough means not only a sufficiency for oneself but what can also be given to one's brothers."

A philosophy of contentment or sufficiency will not be easily implemented in America. It will meet resistance from the well-entrenched philosophy of "more and more" and "bigger and better."

We who make up less than six percent of the world's population consume roughly forty percent of the energy produced annually. The median income of the average white family in America is now fifteen thousand dollars, and that of the average black family is under nine thousand dollars. Both figures are phenomenal in comparison with the lower income in an impoverished country such as India, where the figure falls to less than one hundred and fifty dollars. One hundred and fifty dollars in India will buy roughly what one hundred and fifty dollars will buy in America.

For the average American family to gear down its life-style to the level of the average impoverished Indian family, a Louisville *Courier-Journal* article pointed out, would necessitate dispensing with one or more cars and taking up walking, selling the family house, and throwing away all clothing except a single well-worn garment for each person. It would mean taking up residence in a tent or hovel along the street or on a vacant lot, doing without daily baths, giving up medical and dental care, and eating one subminimal meal per day.

Can any of us imagine what this situation would be like? To shift from a philosophy of continuous upward movement of our economy and life-style to one of voluntary poverty boggles our minds. Two things will strongly resist a change:

One is the fact that our technological society is geared to growth. Technology necessitates more technology. As we have fashioned our society, it will continue to siphon off more and more of the earth's resources, to create greater and greater pollution, and to drive the wedge ever deeper between the rich nations and the poor, our world and the so-called "Third World."

The other resistance to change is something that lies deeper at the root, in our own attachment to things. There is a widespread fallacy that "more and more" will increase our sense of contentment, bring happiness, or lead us to the pot of gold at the end of the rainbow.

But the state of mind in Western society does not confirm this latter conviction. Those who have "more and more" are enjoying what they have "less and less." Acquiring things and gratifying our sensual desires have whetted our desires and appetites rather than satisfied them. They have generated desire without producing a corresponding sense of direction or purpose. Now we find ourselves in the plight of the legendary King Midas. Midas, you recall, had an insatiable desire that everything he touched be turned into gold. It was his misfortune to have his prayer answered, for when he touched his beloved and only daughter, she turned to gold. Too late, Midas discovered that something could be *more* precious than gold.

The question for us is: *Will* we or *can* we learn that something is more precious than the acquisition of "more and more"? Will we be able to discern that the gnawings and cravings within us arise not from physical but from still deeper needs? Will we be able to fathom the meaning of Jesus' declaration, "A human being shall not live by bread alone"?

I am not optimistic. I am not optimistic because I know that we are too capable of self-deception. We are like children who, when they are sleepy, say, "I'm hungry." We have produced a whole generation of compulsive consumers, cravers of "more and more." Yet the deeper craving has been neglected. And we are trying to satisfy it by feeding ourselves on things, as if "more and more" would make the pangs of an empty self disappear. It may be as James said: "You desire and do not have; so you kill. And you covet and cannot obtain; so you fight and wage war. You do not have, because you do not ask. You ask and do not receive, because you ask wrongly, to spend it on your passions" (Jas 4:2-3).

A philosophy of contentment is an urgent concern for our day, therefore. In constructing it, however, we must be sure that we do not posit a merely negative solution to a massive problem. Mere detachment from things will do no more than leave an empty room for seven devils to fill. Our aim has to be the construction of a positive philosophy of use.

The Greeks stated principally the negative side. Aristotle defined the Greek *autarkeia* in terms of self-sufficiency or independence—"to possess all things and to need nothing (or no one)" (*Politics* 7.5). He talked about moderation (*sōphrosynē*), doing "nothing too much." As synonyms of *autarkeia*, the Stoics used the words *apatheia*, detachment, and *eleutheria*, freedom. The wise should never become involved or attached to things or persons. They should always maintain an aloof and noncommittal independence.

Though Paul used the same word, the larger context shows that in all three places in which he used it he meant something quite different. Christians may strive for detachment and possibly even "self-sufficiency," but they do not stop there. Paul's "sufficiency," he makes clear in Philippians 4:10-13, arises out of the conviction that Christ is present to aid in all circumstances in life. "I have strength for all occasions through Christ who gives me strength" (v. 13). This is a better translation than the King James: "I can do all things through Christ which **strengtheneth** me." **Then, as he says in 2 Corinthians 9:8, the Christian's sufficiency is some**thing that we share with others. Contentment means at one and the same time detachment and commitment. I like the way Thomas R. Kelly said it: "He plucks the world out of our hearts, loosening the chains of attachment. And he hurls the world into our hearts, where we and He together carry it in infinitely tender love."[36]

This, you see, strikes at the root of the problem. The root is our anxiety, our little faith, our lack of awareness that God, the heavenly Father, cares. We have to learn, therefore, from the birds and the lilies. They are object lessons to us concerning God's providence. Where anxiety has led us to gluttonous use, faith leads to contentment!

Contentment leads to generous stewardship, our sufficiency supplying those in want. Isn't this the point of Paul's appeal to the Corinthians? "Each one must do as he has made up his mind, not reluctantly or under compulsion, for God loves a cheerful giver. And God is able to provide you with every blessing in abundance, so that you may always have *enough* of everything and may provide in abundance for *every good work*" (2 Cor 9:7-8, italics added).

Let me illustrate this philosophy from Christian history with some examples of persons who laid hold on it in other eras and times.

There were those early Christians who fasted twice a week in order to give food to the poor, who became indentured servants in order to ransom captives and care for the indigent, who sold all their possessions and distributed them to the poor.

There was that vast experiment in voluntary poverty called monasticism. It is true that it was often largely negative, a protest against materialism. Yet, despite its dualism, it produced some truly remarkable examples of self-denial and charity—people such as Anthony, who before age twenty sold and gave away all his property, put his sister in the care of a pious woman, and became a hermit.

There was Francis of Assisi, who, in an age of great inequity in wealth, renounced his family's affluent life-style in order to identify with and minister to the poor. As he put it, he rejected riches in order to "marry Lady Poverty."

There was John Woolman, who, in pre-Revolutionary America, limited his own business in order to travel at his own expense all over the southern colonies to persuade Quakers to free their slaves.

There was Arthur Shearly Cripps, an Anglican missionary to Rhodesia, who died in 1952. He refused to use a conveyance—even a horse, because the natives of Rhodesia did not have access to them. He walked or jogged miles. Every Sunday he jogged miles from his church to a mission station after the morning worship, and then back in the afternoon.

Once, it is said, when he was in his seventies a white man offered him a ride on the ninety-mile trip to Salisbury as he walked with a black friend. He accepted and got in. The white man hurriedly slammed the door to keep the black man from entering. At the end of the ride Cripps turned back down the same road. The driver asked, "Why are you going that way?" "To meet my friend and walk the rest of the way with him," replied Cripps.

In those early Christians, in some of the monks, in Francis of Assisi, and in A. S. Cripps you see the epitome of this philosophy. It involves, first of all, a discovery of the one thing needful that will allow us to detach ourselves from things and share from our sufficiency with those who are in want.

But here we arrive at the more difficult part, the *practice* of contentment. What would this require of us? How would it affect our society and our individual lives?

Socially it would have an enormous impact on our Western life-style —both in detachment and in commitment.

On the negative side, it would mean a reversal of our constant and unflagging drive to increase our gross national product and our national standard of living at the expense of other nations. Some countries have already gone through this type of adjustment. Great Britain is an example. With the gradual sundering of the British Empire, the economy dwindled. In the 1950s and 1960s a Labor government led the British people to tighten their belts as the value of the English pound fell from about five dollars to about half that. Further, the government prepared the nation to enter the European common market, a step that meant sacrifices as well as gains in British production and sales.

This type of shift also means deescalation of the standard of living, which necessitates wiser and better planning of public services. To mention one area only, in Great Britain the government assured fewer automobiles by imposing a prohibitive tax, by imposing tighter fuel controls, and by sustaining public transit facilities in order to avoid the overuse of limited space for constructing bigger and faster highways.

On the positive side, it would mean sharing the wealth and the skills of nations. The United States did this after World War II through the famous Marshall Plan. The British economist Barbara Ward (Lady Jackson) urged the European nations to match the American Marshall plan. It is in the interest of the rich nations to do all within their power to see the poor nations reach their potential, not by exploitation, but by sharing of wealth and know-how. Lady Jackson urged distribution of one percent of the GNP of rich nations among the poor.[37]

But you and I have relatively limited control over the broad social policy. This will change. It is changing. And one could wish more Christian youths would choose the economic field in order to direct the change in the right direction. The answer to the Marxist economic philosophy is a wiser economic policy framed with truly Christian ends in view. This will require wise political action.

Individually, you and I can do more. It is true that there is a kind of economic determinism built into our culture. Advertising has much to do with our thought patterns. It can create a sense of need to the point of servitude. Our streets and highways are glutted with monstrous billboards that testify to the power of the economic motive in our culture.

But, as Christians, is this servitude necessary if we can lay hold on the power of Christ to overcome it? I trust that it is not. Is it not possible for us to take the course of our own lives in hand and to develop a different life-style, one not so dependent on things and one that allows us to exercise Christian stewardship? I believe so. But it will require some serious soul-searching over all that we are now doing. It will require first detachment and then reattachment, God plucking the world out of our hearts and hurling the world into our hearts.

Ask yourself some questions.

First, about detachment. . . .

What *things* control your life? What *things* have you become so dependent upon that you are no longer a free person? Your cars? Your large house? Your boat? Your expensive furniture? Or should I say your mortgages? Your charge accounts? Your credit cards?

Second, about reattachment. . . .

In terms of income and material possessions, compared with the people of most other nations, most of us belong in the affluent category. Supposing that we obtained detachment, contentment, with reference to our possessions and our activities, what will we do with the "surplus" we have now discovered? Will we build new barns to store our greater harvest for our own purposes? Will we go on using all the resources of our world for today? Or will we do as the early Christians did? Will we think about the next generation and the next, about our sons and grandsons?

Our temptation will be to say: "What little bit of extra things I consume will not matter much. Think about what everybody else is doing! I will change my life-style when others do."

This is an admission of our servitude. And I must confess that I am not optimistic regarding a vast shift in our life-style such as I am proposing. Cultural styles are deeply woven into our subconscious patterns of thought. They change when more powerful factors break through to the subconscious. Sometimes violent external upheavals such as wars can effect a change. Whether individuals can break free will depend on the strength of their inner motivation. And, I fear, not many will have the powerful inner compulsion of Francis of Assisi, John Woolman, or Arthur Shearly Cripps.

But the lack of inner motive is not a deficiency that stems from a lack of intellectual comprehension and perception. None of these three men was a part of an intellectual elite, unless, as a poet, Cripps was. They were, on the contrary, simple men with extraordinary intuitive insight that carried them beyond their day. They knew that small efforts matter because God uses them to obtain great ends, just as Romans 8:28 reminds us ever again. Our contentment will have to arise out of our experience of Christ's power within us.

In Summary

In our day, Christian devotion requires a new direction in life-style —toward simplification. Simplification will not occur if we work from the periphery, for our life-styles are programmed into our subconscious patterns of behavior. Some more powerful motive has to break through to the subconscious, erase our sense of satisfaction with our life-styles, and engrave new lines.

Our starting point toward simplification, therefore, lies in "centering down," recovering our own selves in relationship to God. From this Center, perhaps, we will begin to reorder our priorities in the use of time and rediscover how to use things. Some new models are needed. Few of us will reach the plateaus ascended by Francis of Assisi, John Woolman, and Arthur Shearly Cripps; they were horizonal persons. But we can at least run our race of life in the direction they ran, learning in whatever circumstances we find ourselves to be content, having found the power of Christ within us.

Chapter Six

Aids to Meaningful Devotion

The consistent concern of this small book has been the development of a devotional style that will affect the whole of one's life. Ideally the contemplative approach that has been presented would integrate all of one's activities around a God-conscious inner self. This self would then radiate the divine will through both word and deed. Since God is love, love would be in full control.

If this ideal were to be attained, mature Christians might dispense with conventional religious forms and practices. Indeed, they might reach the point where these hindered rather than aided their further growth.

Unfortunately not many, if any, of us reach this level of maturity; so we must give some attention to devotional aids. Our faith and practice require supports and aids, even at the risk of routinizing and overinstitutionalizing them. Failure to discern the necessity of maturation before abandoning forms is one of the grave errors of contemporary antichurch movements. Though their concern with the deadening effects of formalism is legitimate and praiseworthy, by casting aside all forms they have discarded what few aids they had, poor as they may have been, for implementing Christian growth.

The fact is that the history of human religious experience sustains the necessity of discipline. As in athletics, so in spirituality the beginners require conscious discipline, whereas mature persons perform effortlessly because they have mastered the fundamental forms. The point at which one has passed beyond the need for forms is difficult to say, but few, if any, do so.

In an examination of aids to devotion, it may be useful to consider first two widely used but questionable ones—drugs and glossolalia—before looking at those that I can commend unreservedly.

"Mind Expanders"

Mind-expanding or relaxing drugs have been employed for years by some Oriental religions, and such drugs are getting increasing use today. The argument for the use of these drugs seems to be that they break down the barriers imposed by rational and other inhibitions to an experience of transcendence. They expand consciousness. They rearrange patterns of thought and behavior.

To be entirely fair, one must concede the difficulty to which drug users point. Religious persons do have inhibitors that interfere with or forbid the experience of transcendence. Certain beliefs and conventions can stifle openness to reality, even reality observable to the physical senses. They can canonize social injustices on the grounds that the scriptures or faith compel it. Changing these patterns often necessitates extensive education, personal crises, mental and emotional therapy, or other radical means. Experiments have proven that drugs such as LSD can and do effect such changes. They offer a quick solution, whereas other solutions may require years.

The major issue that has to be raised on the other side is whether the dangers resulting from the use of drugs do not outweigh the immediate benefits, assuming that the drugs do what users say. The father of the drug cult, Timothy Leary, has denied vehemently that LSD, if taken in "proper" amounts, is dangerous. Others, likewise, have sustained the safety and nonaddictive quality of "pot," opium, and various narcotics. It is possible, of course, to blame ill effects on *im*proper usage, but there is a growing mass of data that tends to show that drug-taking is dangerous. If it is not inherently dangerous, it becomes so by virtue of our lack of knowledge as to what safe usage would be. Youthful experimenters with LSD now report severe mental and even physical impairment as a result of their "trips." At best, drug experiments, which is basically what this usage should be called, should be restricted in our culture to persons of great emotional maturity.

More is to be gained, I believe, by a disciplined approach to the religious life. It will take longer, but it is possible to cultivate openness within whereby God may penetrate to the subconscious level. If this is to happen, we no doubt will have to alter our life-styles, even our religious life-styles, in order to break down some external barriers. Alteration of life-style is, of course, what will do most to eliminate conditions that are causing profligate drug usage, alcoholism, and other quickie solutions to anxiety, boredom, and fear.

Charismatic Gifts

Another aid to devotion to which substantial numbers of people are attracted is the so-called "baptism of the Holy Spirit," or glossolalia.

The charismatic revival is undoubtedly related to a search for immediate, intuitive apprehension of God in opposition to an over-emphasis on the rational. This seems to me to be substantiated by the fact that the heyday of the tongues movement has occurred since about 1650, the beginning of the Enlightenment, and that it was least prominent in the Middle Ages, when the mystical and intuitive approach dominated.[38]

Contemporary evaluations of glossolalia have been mixed. The fact that the New Testament records the experience, indeed assigns consider-able significance to it (Acts 2; 1 Cor 14), will not allow us to pronounce a purely negative judgment, unless we argue for the temporary character of the gift, viz., for the apostolic age only. Still, even those who have claimed the "gift" express differing opinions as to its meaning. For some it offers continuing sustenance of devotion, for others a passing phenom-enon. Those who have not had the experience can hardly pass judgment on it in regard to its values for others.

The difficulty with speaking in tongues is related less to the phenomenon itself than to claims made for it. Glossolalists frequently see it as the *sine qua non* for all Christians, as *the* spiritual gift par excel-lence, and as the experience that transcends all others. Their desire to impose it as the test of Christianity, as well as negative reactions to it, has resulted in divisions within churches and has caused much turmoil. The hope is that glossolalists will exercise tolerance and remember that there are gifts that Paul, among other early Christians, placed above tongues: the virtues of love, joy, peace, patience, kindness, goodness, faithfulness, gentleness, self-control (Gal 5:22-23); his own calling, that of an apostle, as well as the gift of prophetic powers, etc. (1 Cor 12:28).

Gathering with the Community of Believers

One aid to devotion that is of indisputable value is the community of those who worship God.

In the sixties, as all of us recall, many persons professed a loss of confidence in the institutional church. Today, however, according to a recent national poll, there is a reversal of this trend. The church was listed at the top of institutions in our society in which people do place confidence (sixty-eight percent). This surprising development may be the consequence of a loss of confidence in other institutions, especially in government, but it could also be due to a rediscovery of the true essence of the church.

The church is people, the people of God. The people of God may gather in a variety of ways to express their oneness with one another in Christ. If they function as they should, however, there is maximum potential for growth in spiritual discipline.

The chief aim is laid out well in Paul's prayer for the Philippians: "It is my prayer that your love may grow more and more in knowledge and in every sensitivity, so that you may have a sense of things that matter, in order that you may be pure and blameless for the day of Christ, filled with the fruit of righteousness that redounds through Jesus Christ to the glory and praise of God" (Phil 1:9-11, my translation). The community of believers is the context for developing in the knowledge and skill with which we apply love. The development will not occur automatically. Prayer, Bible study, discussion, and all other aspects of community life should contribute to it. The ultimate aim is, of course, purity of heart and a stock of things that we have done out of love that redound to God's honor and evoke praise from humankind.

Most congregational gatherings as we now experience them probably contribute somewhat to the disciplinary development of the Christian. Many serious Christians, however, are seeking ways to augment what these provide. One possibility is the "house church," gathering in homes or other places for more intimate fellowship, more reflective Bible study, more serious prayer, and pondering God's purposes more deeply. Another is the use of current gatherings, for example, the Sunday school class, for the same purposes. All too often these get trapped in routine discussions that scarcely venture below the surface. We should take care, not to multiply meetings, *but to increase the depth and quality of these for spiritual development.*

Retreats

Another aid to devotion is the retreat, whether private or corporate. Family retreats are also possible.

To seek solitude or to withdraw in times of stress is almost instinctive in human beings, as indeed in most animals. The immense strain under which modern society places most persons makes retreat almost mandatory.

For Christians, however, retreats will be prompted by a quest for communion with the heavenly Father. Thus did Jesus withdraw to fast and pray, evidently not just in the crucial period of vocational search but throughout his ministry. Thus have other great saints withdrawn. For the early monks a deteriorating civilization and even the church did not supply a place for the encounter with God comparable to that which they found in the desert.

Many retreats will be solitary. But the history of religion teaches that it is wise for novices to have retreat leaders, lest they spend their solitude in aimless meandering. Even experienced mystics have sought mentors for special spiritual guidance at such times. The mentor would not always have to be a person, although the greatest aid is probably personal; sometimes the aid might be a retreat manual such as Ignatius Loyola's *Spiritual Exercises* or planned study of the Bible and devotional classics. The purpose of a leader is to lay out some exercises, to evaluate progress, and to offer direction toward further progress.

Corporate retreats, even if they are silent, also need a leader to focus the mind of the group. The leader should obviously be a person of maturity who can challenge the retreatants to proper self-examination and growth. The challenge might be issued through Bible expositions, directed prayers, devotional meditations, individual or group conferences, dialogues, or other means. It is certainly advisable, however, to leave time for private meditation or reflection. In this activistic society of ours, too many retreats are extensions rather than interruptions or diversions of activities. Activities will not cease, but the concern of the retreat should be the cultivation of the contemplative style.

How often and *how long* retreats should be will depend upon the individual or the group and upon their circumstances. Weekend and holiday retreats are becoming increasingly popular. These could occur with some regularity, given the flexibility of work schedules today. Many persons, under stress in times of vocational or family crisis, seek longer retreats for serious contemplation. If financial or other conditions permit, what is to prevent a month-long or even a year-long retreat?

Where retreats occur also will depend upon the individual or the group and their circumstances. There are today a large number of private, church, and public retreat facilities, such as parks. For most persons, cost as well as accessibility will determine which of these one uses. The ecumenical spirit of the times makes it unnecessary to find retreat facilities in one's own denomination. The writer's most significant retreats, for example, have taken place in a Roman Catholic monastery that graciously provides however much or little direction one wishes. Likewise, he directed a retreat of college youths with very diverse backgrounds on an army reservation camping facility.

The Bible and Other Devotional Literature

Another aid to devotion is literature. For many Protestants this may be the Bible alone, for the Reformers made us "the people of one book." Many Christians, however, are discovering that the reading of the Bible alone frequently becomes so routine that it loses all significance. Consequently, they seek to enhance their commitment to God through other literature that has devotional value and that opens up vast new insights regarding the spiritual life. What does this literature include?

The most obvious selections are the classics of Christian devotion: Augustine's *Confessions*, Bernard of Clairvaux's *On the Love of God*, Thomas á Kempis' *The Imitation of Christ, The Little Flowers of St. Francis*, John of the Cross's *Dark Night of the Soul*, Blaise Pascal's *Pensées*, John Bunyan's *The Pilgrim's Progress*, William Law's *A Serious Call to a Devout and Holy Life*, John Woolman's *Journal*, and Søren Kierkegaard's *Purity of Heart*—among others.

To these, however, one should add some modern devotional writings that vie for a place of honor among the classics: Thomas R. Kelly's *Testament of Devotion*; Dietrich Bonhöffer's *Letters and Papers from Prison*; Father Alfred Delp's *Prison Meditations*; Thomas Merton's *Seven Storey Mountains*, and Teilhard de Chardin's *Divine Milieu*.[39]

There are also collections of prayers that teach us much not only about prayer but about spirituality in general: John Baillie's *A Diary of Private Prayer*, Thomas Merton's *Thoughts in Solitude*, Michel Quoist's *Prayers*, and Malcolm Boyd's *Are You Running with Me, Jesus*?

Many other types of literature that have no particular devotional slant may also aid devotion by inspiring new insights and guiding thoughts. One could compose a long list of writings. It will suffice, however, to name a few as examples.

Recent *biographical* writings that I have found helpful include: Irving Stone's *The Agony and the Ecstasy*, a novelized biography of Michelangelo; Albert Schweitzer's autobiographical *Out of My Life and Thought*; Roland Bainton's *Here I Stand*, a biography of Martin Luther, and *Erasmus of Christendom*; Eberhard Bethge's *Dietrich Bonhöffer*; Langdon Gilkey's *Shantung Compound*; Albert Speer's autobiographical *Inside the Third Reich*; Jan De Hartog's *The Peaceable Kingdom*; and Douglas Steere's *God's Irregular: Arthur Shearly Cripps*.

Other types of *prose* or *poetry* may likewise provoke and stimulate us to deepen our level of spirituality: William Goldiam Golding's *Lord of the Flies*; Alan Paton's *Cry, the Beloved Country*; Thomas Merton's *Figures for an Apocalypse* and *The Geography of Lograire*.

Some *general writings* about contemporary life have also opened windows for some: Charles Reich's *The Greening of America*, Alvin Toffler's *Future Shock*, Theodore Roszak's *The Making of a Counter-Culture* and *Where the Wasteland Ends*, and Wayne E. Oates' *Confessions of a Workaholic*.

From what has been said, it will be evident that the range of possibilities is immense. Limitations will be imposed by one's ability, desire, or time to read. With such a supermarket, all, of course, will need some guidelines to follow. In *Seekers After Mature Faith*, I set forth partially some rules regarding the reading of classics. They are applicable to other devotional reading.

1. *Select carefully*. Not all devotional or other writings employed for that purpose are useful to everyone. It is wise to make a wide survey and then to settle on those that promise the most fruit for you. Older writings need to be chosen with particular care, for their datedness may pose problems of interest that require special effort to resolve. If we are not willing to put forth the necessary effort, we may not find them edifying.

2. *Read carefully, mark, and reread.* Most classical works are worth reading with greater care and even again in order to let their insights take full effect. Haphazard repetitive reading may dull the effect, but careful concentrated reading will usually open remarkable new insights. To assure full concentration, we should probably read at set times for brief periods until our powers of concentration reach their maximum.

To avoid losing rich passages, it is helpful to mark them. Unless books have full indexes, moreover, we ought to make a kind of private index on the flyleaf or elsewhere. Thus, when we return, we will have some additional assistance in our search for more insightful passages.

3. *Read critically and yet sympathetically.* All literature, even the Bible, should be read critically. It will not do to gloss over difficulties. Some persons, I am aware, think that critical reading may destroy or diminish the inspiration derived from the reading. That would be true, however, only if one were doing the reading simply as a critical exercise. Critical reading entails learning all one can about the author, date, place of writing, purpose, and so on. Every writing should be interpreted contextually.

Nevertheless, criticism should be balanced by sympathetic attention to the authors. The goal is to identify with them in their personal experience in such a way that insights from that are channeled into *our* experiences. For some works, particularly modern ones, this will occur naturally and effortlessly. The writers' experiences will mesh perfectly with ours. But for many other works this will not be the case until we have become truly acquainted with the authors themselves, and that may take a long time.

Visuals

Another aid to devotion is visual—plays, movies, paintings, sculptures, and other objects of art. Indeed, the contemporary era is characterized by a shift from audio to video that has altered both the way we learn and our self-understanding. By virtue of the development of television in particular, we now experience remote happenings not merely by ear but by both ear and eye. Immediate experience, of course, can cut two ways—deadening perception by overexposure or enhancing it by immediacy. This means that here too we will cultivate selective viewing.

Plays and movies may inspire some persons even more than books, by virtue of fuller involvement. There are few religious playwrights whose works have gained a wide audience, but many important popular plays and movies have religious overtones, for example, the musicals *Jesus Christ Superstar* and *Godspell; Brother Sun, Sister Moon;* and *The Poseidon Adventure.* This fact indicates that one should stay alive to possible situations in which God may disclose God's self and God's purposes to us more fully.

Paintings, sculptures, and other art forms have long been used as aids to devotion. Indeed, the use of images has been the essence of Eastern Christian worship. Protestantism has experienced a famine here by reason of a virtually total accent upon oral communication. In the Reformation, to be sure, this was sensible, for the invention of printing was causing a transformation of communication comparable to what is now happening *vis-a-vis* the mass media. Now, however, we need badly to catch up with the new revolution in communications.

There is a wealth of classical Christian art that still inspires many. From the middle of the nineteenth century on, however, art has focused on more secular concerns. Still many great paintings—for instance, those of Dali, Goya, and Picasso—have deep religious as well as human significance. And in recent years there has been some revival of religious art, sculpture, architecture, and the like. A specimen that combines all of these is Coventry Cathedral in England. This cathedral, largely destroyed by bombs during World War II, merged medieval and modern in architecture, stained-glass windows, baptistery, crosses, tapestry, and other things.

Audials

Another aid to worship is audial—music, addresses, sermons, and varied other sounds.

Protestants, as I said above, have always emphasized these. The electronic age has expanded greatly the possibilities, if one is wise enough to be selective. Unfortunately most of us are probably suffering from a surfeit of sound—so much so that specialists in hearing now warn of possible impairment of hearing from excessive noise. Noise pollution will have to be dealt with as a major social problem if there is to be any help.

Nevertheless, many forms of sound could aid devotion. Music, for instance, has long been thought to be very near to contemplation itself. Much of the world's great music, moreover, is religious music. The lyrics of great hymns obviously present opportunities for God to open insights, but tunes may convey powerful feeling that rises beyond the level of formal speech.

Addresses and sermons aid devotion. This is obviously a direct purpose of the sermon, but other addresses might do the same thing. Recording on discs and tapes now makes great speeches and sermons available to a larger audience and to private as well as corporate hearers. A fine sermon specimen is Martin Luther King's "I Have a Dream."

The development of the media has also enabled us to avail ourselves of sounds of nature or other elements of our experience that might otherwise be denied. These will never substitute for the direct contact with nature through which God sometimes enters our immediate experience, but they could help to establish a mood.

Kinetic Arts

Another aid to devotion that has sometimes been employed by religious persons is the dance. Dancing is referred to a number of times in the Old Testament, either in connection with private expressions of joy (2 Sam 6:14) or public worship (Ps 149:3; Jer 31:13). The early Christians prohibited dancing because of the pagan use of it for lewd and obscene purposes. Some Christians, however, have revived it in worship. The Shakers, despite their puritanism, for example, made it a central feature of their worship, working out elaborate patterns with eschatological nuances.

Many youth today express joy, thanksgiving, and commitment to God through dancing of one type or another. The body control that certain dances require could function somewhat like yoga exercises, as an aid to concentration and discipline of the mind.

Asceticism

Another aid to devotion that has played a significant role in the history of most religions is asceticism—fasting or otherwise denying oneself. Jesus fasted, his criticisms of the Pharisaic regulations notwithstanding. So did his early followers (Acts 14:23, 27:9; 2 Cor 6:5, 11:27). Fasting or other ascetic practices became a key element in monastic piety. Unfortunately excesses occurred that caused monasticism to be criticized and gradually abandoned by Protestants. The truth is that monastic asceticism got sidetracked from the original purposes of fasting because of the dualism of the times. Doing ascetic exercises was seen as a way of showing contempt for the physical or material aspect of humanity, which was considered evil. Hermits especially engaged in ridiculous extremes of self-mortification. Simeon Stylites, for example, perched atop a pillar in the desert of Syria laden with chains for thirty years. He stood all night motionless with his hands outstretched toward heaven or touched his forehead with his feet 1,244 times in succession. He refused to bathe until vermin dropped from his body.

There is, however, a legitimate role for fasting as self-discipline and, more positively, to share what is left over with persons in need, as early Christians did. Overindulgence and shameful waste are not uncommon in American life. Such things undoubtedly detract from the disciplined life. Too much food, as the early Christians and modern yogis insist, causes not only physical but also mental and spiritual sluggishness. Moderation in eating would reverse this process. The object is, as ascetics have sought throughout history, to attain fullness of life through a healthy interaction of mind and body.[40]

How much and how often should a Christian fast? Since I have experimented with this only in a limited way, I cannot fill out a definite prescription. For anyone not accustomed to fasting, it would be wise to start denying oneself gradually. Most of us could delete one meal a day for an experimental period, for instance, and see whether more would be feasible. Monastic history has taught that crash programs do little more than destroy personal health. The rule should be: Eat what one requires for robust health but avoid overeating. Then, voluntarily give the excess to those who are in need.

Keeping a Journal

Another aid to devotion, which the early Quakers popularized, is the keeping of a diary or journal. The journals of George Fox, John Woolman, John Wesley, Dag Hammarskjöld, Thomas Merton, and others constitute some of our premier devotional classics.

The journal should be, not a log of activities, though it may include a record of these but, a personal inventory. This type of record allows room to incorporate observations about spiritual growth that can be referred to later. Thomas Merton, who preferred the journal to other styles of religious writing, jotted down observations about what he read, about persons he met, about individual needs and experiences, about his own community, about American society, and about miscellaneous inspirations. These should be composed for one's personal edification rather than for a larger readership. This will assure that they will be more intimate and analytical. There is, of course, always some problem as to *how* intimate, which we must each solve for ourselves. We should be open and honest with ourselves, but we may not want to record every errant thought.

Journals are meant to be read and reread occasionally by their composers in order to measure spiritual development. We may surprise ourselves, upon later reading, at the depth of some insights. A private diary may edify in much the same way that a journal written by someone else will.

Aids as Approximates, Not Ultimates

Before concluding this chapter, I must lay down a warning about the substitution of the aids for God. Such is the risk that religious exercises of any type always run.

Some sincere Christians have argued, for this reason, that Christianity should abandon all religious exercises. In support, they cite passages from the prophets about God's hatred of feasts, new moons, sabbaths, and the rest, and Jesus' critique of the religious observances of Judaism.

As persuasive as this concern is, however, one must ask whether many persons can do without more or less formal religious exercises.

Indeed, was the critique of Israel's religion by the prophets and by Jesus a denunciation and repudiation of all religious forms or of their abuse? The fact that both the prophets and Jesus made use of religious exercises of all types surely sustains the latter answer. Their protest was that religious exercises should be means and not become ends in themselves.

Still, the danger remains. Whether it can be avoided is debatable. Certainly avoidance of it will require continuous vigilance and reminders about the danger. It is a risk that will have to be run.

Notes

[1]Edmund Leach, "We Scientists Have a Right to Play God," *Look* (December 1968).

[2]Conference on "The Habitable City," Centre College, Danville KY, reported in *The Louisville Times,* 16 October 1969, A 13.

[3]See my article, A Rationale for Baptist Higher Education," *Search* 4 (Fall 1973):11-21.

[4]Augustine, *The Confessions of St. Augustine,* trans. John K. Ryan (Garden City NJ: Doubleday & Company, Inc., Image Books, 1960) 1.1.1.

[5]See, e.g., Roger Garaudy, *The Crisis in Communism* (Grove Press, Inc., 1972) and his *Marxism in the 20th Century* (New York: Charles Scribner's Sons, 1970).

[6]Thomas Merton, *Faith and Violence* (South Bend IN: University of Notre Dame Press, 1968) 216.

[7]See Thomas Merton, "Christian Culture Needs Oriental Wisdom," *Catholic World,* 195 (May 1962): 72-79.

[8]Alvin Toffler, *Future Shock* (New York: Bantam Books, Inc., 1970) 26.

[9]Dietrich Bonhoeffer, *Letters and Papers from Prison,* ed. Eberhard Bethge, trans. Reginald H. Fuller, rev. ed. (New York: Macmillan Company, 1967) 167 ff.

[10]Allen R. Brockway, *The Secular Saint* (Garden City NJ: Doubleday & Company, Inc., 1968) 92, 105.

[11]Father Alfred Delp, *Prison Meditations* (New York: Macmillan Company, 1963) 93.

[12]Max Planck, *Scientific Autobiography* (Philosophical Library, 1949) 139 ff.

[13]Malcolm Muggeridge, *Jesus Rediscovered* (London: William Collins Sons & Co., Ltd., 1967).

[14]See Harvey Cox, *The Feast of Fools* (San Francisco: Harper & Row Publishers, Inc., 1969) and Cox's recent article "From Bullhorn to the Bible," Louisville KY, *Courier-Journal and Times,* 6 May 1973, 6.

[15]Claude Cuenot, *Teilhard de Chardin* (Baltimore: Helicon Press, Inc., 1965) 14.

[16]Pierre Teilhard de Chardin, *Letters from a Traveller*, 1923–1955 (London: William Collins Sons & Co., Ltd., 1956) 61.

[17]Charles Reich, *The Greening of America* (New York: Random House, Inc., 1970).

[18]H. Richard Niebuhr, *The Purpose of the Church and Its Ministry* (New York: Harper & Brothers, 1956).

[19]Lin Yutang, *From Pagan to Christian* (Avon Books, 1959) 212.

[20]Teilhard de Chardin, *Letters from a Traveller*, 1923–1955, 119-20.

[21]Dennis V. White, "The Success 'Rat Race' Seems to Be Slowing," *Louisville Times*, 26 July 1973, 43.

[22]Thomas Merton, *Faith and Violence* (South Bend IN: University of Notre Dame Press, 1968) 223.

[23]Thomas Merton, *The Asian Journal of Thomas Merton* (New Directions, 1973).

[24]Judy Rosenfeld, "What Is 'TM' and Does It Bring Inner Peace?" Louisville KY, *Courier-Journal,* 5 June 1972.

[25]Pierre Teilhard de Chardin, *The Divine Milieu* (New York: Harper Brothers, 1960) 55 f.

[26]Joachim Jeremias, *Abba. Studien zur neutestamentliche Theologie und Zeitgeschichte* (Gottingen: Vandenhoeck & Ruprecht, 1966) 15-67.

[27]Augustine, *The Confessions of St. Augustine*, trans. John K. Ryan, 1.1, 43.

[28]Robert J. Donovan, "The Root of Evil: Today's Blah Life," *The Louisville Times*, 28 September 1971, A7.

[29]Augustine, *Soliloquies,* 1.1-6.

[30]Michel Quoist, *Prayers,* trans. Angus M. Forsyth and Anne Marie de Commaille (New York: Sheed & Ward, Inc., 1963) 114f. Used by permission.

[31]Morton Kelsey, *Healing and Christianity* (San Francisco: Harper & Row, Publishers, Inc., 1973).

[32]Thomas R. Kelly, *A Testament of Devotion* (London: Hodder & Stoughton, Ltd., 1941) 68.

[33]Thomas Merton, *The Asian Journal of Thomas Merton* (New Directions, 1973) 103.

[34]Wayne E. Oates, *Confessions of a Workaholic* (World Publishing Company, 1971).

[35]Gerhard Kittel, "*Arkeō, et al.*" *Theological Dictionary of the New Testament*, 10 vols. (Grand Rapids: Wm. B. Eerdmans Publishing Company, 1964) 1: 467.

[36]Thomas R. Kelly, *A Testament of Devotion*, 43f.

[37]Barbara Ward (Lady Jackson) *The Rich Nations and the Poor Nations* (New York and London: W. W. Norton & Company, Inc., 1962).

[38]See my essay in Watson E. Mills (ed.), *Speaking in Tongues: Let's Talk About It* (Waco TX: Word, Inc., 1973).

[39]I have discussed most of these books in my introduction to the devotional classics, *Seekers After Mature Faith* (Waco TX: Word Books, 1968).

[40]See Margaret Miles, *Fullness of Life: Historical Foundations for a New Asceticism.* (Philadelphia: Westminster Press, 1981).

Selected Devotional Reading

I. Devotional Classics

(in chronological sequence)

Augustine (354–430), *The Confessions of St. Augustine*, trans. John K. Ryan. Doubleday & Company, Inc., Image Books, 1960. Composed around A.D. 397-400. An all-time favorite.

Bernard of Clairvaux (1091–1153), *On the Love of God*, in *Late Medieval Mysticism,* The Library of Christian Classics, Vol. XIII, ed. Ray C. Petry. Westminster Press, 1957. Pp. 54-65.

Thomas á Kempis (1380–1471), *Of the Imitation of Christ*, trans. Abbot Justin McCann. The New American Library of World Literature, Inc., Mentor-Omega Books, 1957.

John of the Cross (1542–1591), *Dark Night of the Soul*, trans. E. Allison Peers. Garden City NY: Doubleday Image Books, 1959.

Teresa of Avila (1515–1582), *Auto-biography*, trans. E. Allison Peers. Garden City NY: Doubleday Image Books, 1960. A wonderful mine of insight about prayer.

Brother Lawrence (Nicholas Hermann, 1611–1691), *The Practice of the Presence of God.* Fleming H. Revell Company, 1895. A simple, straightforward approach to the religious life.

Blaise Pascal (1623–1662), *Pensées*, trans. H. F. Stewart. Modern Library, Inc. n.d. A bilingual edition. Notes for an apology for Christianity that was never written.

John Bunyan (1628–1688), *The Pilgrim's Progress*. The New American Library of World Literature, Inc., Signet Classic, 1964. A modernization.

William Law (1686–1761), *A Serious Call to a Devout and Holy Life*. Wm. B. Eerdmans Publishing Company, 1966. A challenging argument for discipline in prayer and devotional activities.

John Woolman (1720–1772), *The Journal of John Woolman and A Plea for the Poor*. John Greenleaf Whittier ed. text. Citadel Press, 1972.

Søren Kierkengaard (1813–1855), *Purity of Heart*, trans. Douglas V. Steere. Harper & Brothers, Harper Torchbooks, 1956.

Thomas R. Kelly (1893–1941), *A Testament of Devotion*. Harper & Row, Publishers, Inc. 1971. A Quaker classic with highly relevant insights for the modern day. A favorite of students.

Dietrich Bonhöffer (1906–1945), *Letters and Papers from Prison*, enlarged ed., ed. Eberhard Bethge. Macmillan Company, 1972. Personal letters added to the well-known classic.

_____, *The Cost of Discipleship*. Macmillan Company, 1953. A challenging theological work.

_____, *Life Together*, trans. John W. Doberstein. New York & Evamston: Harper & Row, Publishers, 1954. A treatise on community as preparation for resistance to the Nazis.

Alfred Delp (d. 1945), *The Prison Meditations of Father Alfred Delp*. The Macmillan Company, 1963. Sermons and letter composed before his execution by the Nazis.

Dag Hammarskjöld (1905–1961), *Markings*, trans. W. H. Auden and Leif Sjoberg. London: Faber & Faber, Ltd., 1964. Jottings by the onetime Secretary-General of the United Nations. Sometimes mysterious and poetic. Needs to be read with the background in Henry P. Van Dusen, *Dag Hammarskjöld: The Statesman and HisFaith*, rev. ed. Harper & Row, Publishers, Inc., Colophon Books, 1967, or in Gustaf Aulen, *Dag Hammarskjöld's White Book: The Meaning of Markings*. Fortress Press, 1969.

Pierre Teilhard de Chardin (1881–1955), *Letters from a Traveler*. Harper & Row, Publishers, Inc., 1962. Selected letters that show the development of his theological thought.

_____, *The Divine Milieu: An Essay on the Interior Life*. Harper & Brothers, 1960. A penetrating essay on spirituality.

Thomas Merton (1915–1968), *The Seven Storey Mountain*. Harcourt, Brace and Company, Inc., 1948. Merton's early spiritual biography.

_____, *Contemplative Prayer*. Garden City NY: Doubleday Image Books, 1971.

_____, *New Seeds of Contemplation*. New York: New Directions, 1961.

Douglas V. Steere (1901–), *Gleanings*. Nashville: The Upper Room, 1986. A collection including biographical essay and the classic *On Listening to Another*.

II. Collections of Prayers

Baillie, John, *A Diary of Private Prayer*. Oxford University Press, 1936. More traditional, phrased in biblical language, theologically perceptive.

Barclay, William, *A Book of Everyday Prayers*. Harper & Brothers, 1960.

Boyd, Malcolm, *Are You Running with Me, Jesus*? Holt, Rinehart & Winston, Inc., 1965. Very popular prayers in colloquial style.

Kepler, Thomas S., *Leaves from a Spiritual Notebook*. Abingdon Press, 1960.

Kierkegaard, Søren, *The Prayers of Kierkegaard*, ed. Perry D. LeFevre. University of Chicago Press, 1956.

Merton, Thomas, *Thoughts in Solitude*. Doubleday & Company, Inc., Image Books, 1968. A monk's reflections about the devout life.

Quoist, Michel, *Prayers*, trans. Angus M. Forsyth and Anne Marie de Commaille. Sheed & Ward, Inc., 1963. Poetic prayers of immense depth by the French abbot.

Rauschenbusch, Walter, *Prayers of the Social Awakening*. Pilgrim Press, 1960. Still relevant prayers composed for the "social gospel" movement.

III. Biographical and Autobiographical Writings

Bainton, Roland, *Erasmus of Christendom*. Charles Scribner's Sons, 1969.

_____, *Here I Stand: A Life of Martin Luther*. Abingdon-Cokesbury Press, 1950.

Bethge, Eberhard, *Dietrich Bonhöffer: Man of Vision, Man of Courage*, trans. Eric Mosbacher *et al.* Harper & Row, Publishers, Inc. 1970.

Cuenot, Claude, *Teilhard de Chardin*, trans. Vincent Colimore. Helicon Press, Inc., 1965.

De Hartog, Jan, *The Peaceable Kingdom*. Atheneum Publishers, 1971.

Gilkey, Langdon, *Shantung Compound*. Harper & Row, Publishers, Inc., 1966.

Kelly, Richard M., *Thomas Kelly: A Biography*. Harper & Row, 1966.

Sabatier, Paul, *Life of St. Francis of Assisi*, trans. Louise Seymour Hough-
    ton. London: Hodder & Stoughton, Ltd., 1894.
Schweitzer, Albert, *Out of My Life and Thought: An Autobiography*,
    trans. C. T. Campion. The New American Library of World Liter-
    ature, Inc., 1949.
Speer, Albert, *Inside the Third Reich*, trans. Richard and Clara Winston.
    Avon Books, 1971.
Steere, Douglas V., *God's Irregular, Arthur Shearly Cripps: A Rhodesian
    Epic*. London: S. P. C. K., 1973.
Stone, Irving, *The Agony and the Ecstasy: A Novel of Michelangelo*.
    Doubleday & Company, Inc. 1961.
Toynbee, Arnold, *Experiences*. Oxford University Press, 1969.

IV. Miscellaneous Writings

Golding, William, *Lord of the Flies: A Novel*. Coward-McCann, Inc.,
    1962.
_____, *The Spire*. Harcourt, Brace & World, Inc., 1964.
Merton, Thomas, *Conjectures of a Guilty Bystander*. Doubleday & Com-
    pany, Inc., Image Books, 1968.
_____, *Figures for an Apocalypse*. New Directions, 1947.
_____, *The Geography of Lograire*. New Directions, 1969.
_____, *No Man Is an Island*. Doubleday & Company, Inc., Image Books,
    1967.
Oates, Wayne E., *Confessions of a Workaholic*. World Publishing Com-
    pany, 1971.
Reich, Charles A., *The Greening of America*. Bantam Books, Inc., 1970.
Roszak, Theodore, *The Making of a Counter-Culture: Reflections on the
    Technocratic Society and Its Youthful Opposition*. Doubleday &
    Company, Inc., 1969.
_____, *Where the Wasteland Ends: Politics and Transcendence in Post-
    industrial Society*. Doubleday & Company, Inc., 1972.

V. Journals

Weavings. Published monthly by The Upper Room, 1908 Grand Avenue,
    P. O. Box 189, Nashville TN 37202. 1986–.